Couples Therapy

Real and Proven Strategies to Connect, Find Intimacy and Restore Your Relationship - Includes Questions for Couples and Healing from Infidelity

Wanda Kelly

©Copyright 2021 – Wanda Kelly - All rights reserved

The content contained within this book may not be reproduced, duplicated, or transmitted without direct written permission from the author or the publisher.

Under no circumstances will any blame or legal responsibility be held against the publisher, or author, for any damages, reparation, or monetary loss due to the information contained within this book, either directly or indirectly.

Legal Notice

This book is copyright protected. This book is only for personal use. You cannot amend, distribute, sell, use, quote or paraphrase any part, or the content within this book, without the consent of the author-publisher.

Disclaimer Notice

Please note the information contained within this document is for educational and entertainment purposes only. All effort has been executed to present accurate, up to date, and reliable, complete information. No warranties of any kind are declared or implied. Readers acknowledge that the author is not engaging in the rendering of legal, financial, medical, or professional advice.

Table of Contents

Anxiety in Relationships 5

Introduction 6
Chapter 1: What is anxiety and how to recognize it 10
Chapter 2: How Anxiety Starts in a Relationship 16
Chapter 3: Insecurity in relationships 22
Chapter 4: Self-Evaluation of Anxiety in a Relationship 36
Chapter 5: Practical Strategies to Solving Anxiety Issues in a Relationship 49
Chapter 6: How to Help Your Partner If They Suffer from Relationship Anxiety 56
Chapter 7: What is jealousy, how to overcome it, what are the symptoms, and how to build trust in the relationship 67
Chapter 8: How to eliminate negative thinking and the fear of abandonment 80
Chapter 9: How to resolve conflicts and save your relationship (especially in marriage) 96
Conclusion 105

Questions for Couples 108

Introduction 109
Chapter 1: Questions on Trust 115
Chapter 2: Questions on Communication 126
Chapter 3: Questions on Fun 139
Chapter 4: Questions on Respect 147
Chapter 5: Questions on Quality time 158
Chapter 6: Questions on How to fight fair 165
Chapter 7: Questions That Make you Think 175

Chapter 8: Questions on Conflicts with In-laws and Extended Family Members 186

Chapter 9: Questions on Money Matters 193

Chapter 10: Questions on Intimacy 200

Chapter 11: Questions on Reconnecting with Your Spouse 207

Chapter 12: Day-to-day Conflict Resolution 215

Conclusion 220

Healing from Infidelity 222

Introduction 223

Chapter 1: Understanding Infidelity 227

Chapter 2: Protecting your Marriage and Family from Infidelity 233

Chapter 3: Facilitators of Cheating 237

Chapter 4: Psychology of Cheating 249

Chapter 5: Various Types of Infidelity 260

Chapter 6: How to Avoid Divorce due to Infidelity 268

Chapter 7: Are Adultery and Infidelity the Same? 276

Chapter 8: Preventing the Reoccurrence of Infidelity 289

Chapter 9: Meditation for Healing 295

Chapter 10: Do's and Don'ts After Discovering Infidelity 298

Chapter 11: The Rebuilding Process 305

Chapter 12: Healing from Infidelity in LGBTQ Couples 312

Chapter 13: Tips for Re-building Trust with your Partner 321

Bonus Test: The Perfect Test to Find Out if Your Partner Is Cheating on You 326

Conclusion 331

Anxiety in Relationships

How to Stop Feeling Insecure and Worrying in a Relationship

Introduction

Anxiety is a part of all life activities; it is also a universal and emotional feeling. Its natural function is to alert us of possible threats so that we can assess them accurately and respond to them effectively. This increased preparation can also enable people to boost their efficiency and enhance innovative drives. Anxiety is also seen as a contemporary societal phenomenon and is reflected more and more in the arts, music, literature, and social media. Anxiety induces excessive or exaggerated reactions to potential risks, leading to chronic and debilitating symptoms related to anxiety disorganizations like fear, phobia, and repetitive behaviors, which also undermine other people's lives.

Anxiety is a normal human condition and a necessary part of our lives. We all have a trait of anxiety in one way or the other. In "fight or flight mode," fear allows us to recognize and respond to hazards. This will inspire us to face tough challenges. The 'right' level of fear will enable us to do more and inspire innovations and practices. Yet anxiety can be viewed from another perspective. Persistent anxiety caused by significant emotional discomfort can lead to unease and, at worst, cause disturbances such as fear, phobia, and obsession. At this point, anxiety may have profoundly distressing and poor effects on our lives and our physical and mental health.

The sense of widespread fear is supported by an investigation commissioned by the Mental Health Foundation. Disturbingly, almost 1 in 5 people have been revealed to have active anxiety "almost every day" or "almost all the time." The study indicates that 'finance, expenses, and debt' are the most common causes of anxiety and perhaps represents the effect of unemployment and inflation on public health and wellness. Moreover, half of the population has reported that 'people are more depressed than they were five years ago.' Anxiety is among the most widely identified, under-diagnosed, and under-treated conditions within the mental health community. The ability to cope with anxiety is the secret to survival in the face of life. However, knowing it too often means that we risk losing our real self, finding a balance, or relaxing and healing in our lives. We can never be more important to our well-being if we only seek some inner harmony.

This study discusses anxiety as a central component of our nature and part of the natural reaction to human emotions.

This is also a challenge to the stigma, which still prevents us from finding support and assistance when our anxiety is becoming a real issue. As individuals and communities, we need to fully understand and participate in anxiety programs, identify the warnings in ourselves and ensure that we have methods to manage it when it tends to harm our emotions. We have to consider if others around us, like friends, relatives, and colleagues, suffer from or are at risk of distressing anxiety due to life events and circumstances. Community public health initiatives have to identify areas of high anxiety and include a continuum of assistance that is non-stigmatic and easy to access. To identify the best places and alliances for those 1 out of 5 people who have problems almost often or always, we urge public health commissioners to look at the list of common online survey sources and use them as a parameter. I believe that public policy will benefit significantly from "fear consciousness" and changing its policies and modes of public interaction to avoid and reduce anxiety. If we honestly understand the rising costs for individuals, their future children, families, and employers with anxiety, we need to act now. This is one of the bases of this book.

It takes a while to stop worrying and keep our anxious thoughts under strict control. Often these thoughts leave us, and we start feeling overwhelmed. Other people have chronic anxiety, leading to daily physical symptoms that are unpleasant or even distressing. These symptoms may grow and cause limiting effects on our lives. Fear can cause these feelings too. Turning to worrisome circumstances can unbalance us, but getting through them can positively affect our lives.

Anxiety will work either for us or against us in an emotional state. It's something that we all share but varies from person to person based on how we experience joy and respond to it. Our lives, education, and personalities all can influence an individual's behavior towards fear during an experience.

Becoming depressed is not a sign of weakness, but anyone under these symptoms needs to see a counselor or a psychiatrist.

Yet, once you begin to better understand anxiety, you can do a lot to reduce the pressure and learn to feel the full spectrum of emotions without thinking about them.

Chapter 1:
What is anxiety and how to recognize it

Anxiety is your mind and body's natural reaction to stressful or dangerous situations. It is a normal response that we all experience at one time or another throughout our lives. However, when an anxiety disorder exists, it can take a heavy toll, both mentally and physically. Anxiety disorders are characterized by excessive fear of real or imagined events that can cause minor or drastic changes in a person's life.

One of the most common symptoms is what's known as an anxiety attack, which a person can experience even when they aren't facing any immediate danger. When something triggers an anxiety attack, the person will usually experience feelings of panic, accompanied by physical symptoms such as sweaty palms, trembling, nausea, elevated heart rate, pain, and difficulty breathing. Anxiety attacks aren't permanent and usually last anywhere from a few minutes to a few hours.

People of all ages can suffer from anxiety disorders, and there are many different causes and triggers for them. For example, the most common reasons for anxiety in children and teens are the pressure to do well in school, bullying from classmates or teachers, sibling rivalry, and upcoming exams. Many young children also face separation anxiety, which happens when the child gets permanently or temporarily separated from one or both parents.

For adults, the causes of anxiety disorders tend to be work-related. Other common reasons for anxiety include traumatic events, the need to meet expectations or fear of failure.

These situations exert immense pressure on the person's psyche, and their fear levels rise as a result. Their mental health suffers, and they begin to do poorly in school or work.

In addition to psychological damage, their physical health will take a hit as well. Stomach problems, erratic heart rate, shortness of breath, nausea, sleeping disorders, and fatigue are all physical manifestations of an anxiety disorder.

There are plenty of things you can do if you or the people close to you display symptoms of an anxiety disorder. Psychotherapy is the best course of action if you see signs of depression or anxiety in yourself or your loved ones. Depending on the severity of the symptoms, a psychiatrist might also prescribe medication. Anti-anxiety medication can provide quick and effective relief from panic attacks, as well as long-term stability. Your psychiatrist will manage the dosage of these treatments and make adjustments as you progress.

Anxiety disorders can further be classified into the following types:

•Generalized Anxiety Disorder (GAD) is a type of anxiety disorder in which a person endures a constant state of stress and depression without any apparent problems or stressors.

People suffering from generalized anxiety disorder find it difficult to sleep and relax their minds. Common symptoms of GAD include shortness of breath, headaches, muscle pain, nausea, trembling, sweating, irritability, and lightheadedness.

•Panic Disorder (PD) is a severe type of anxiety disorder that causes excessive and unexpected terror, which keeps the individual in a state of near-constant fear. This type of anxiety disorder makes the individual unable to make any life decisions. A person with Panic Disorder usually avoids specific situations that can trigger a panic attack. Significant panic disorder symptoms include sweating, trembling, shortness of breath, lightheadedness, GAD, headaches, muscle pain, chest pain, and increased heart rate. People who have Panic Disorder can have a significant fear of sudden death or losing their mental health. Drug abuse, depression, and alcoholism are common problems among people living with PD.

•Agoraphobia is a type of anxiety disorder in which the individual restricts themselves from performing daily activities to the point where they stay indoors for weeks or even months. This is because of their fear, whether real or perceived, of feeling trapped or helpless in a public setting, be it standing in a queue, getting on public transport, or being in a crowd. In this way, they believe they can avoid any situations that can trigger a panic attack.

•Social Anxiety is a type of anxiety disorder that is mostly triggered in social events and gatherings. It stems from the fear of being humiliated or rejected by other people. This makes the individual stay away from parties, dinners, or any social gatherings where the person feels that they will be scrutinized. It is important to note that Social Anxiety is not the same thing as shyness.

Social Anxiety can adversely affect the individual's relationships with their loved ones. It drives a wedge between them and those who love them and want to help them overcome this disorder. That's why it's vital to discuss anxiety symptoms with loved ones. Timely and effective treatment is crucial for people with Social Anxiety to recover their relationships and social life.

•Obsessive-Compulsive Disorder (OCD) is a condition in which the individual becomes unable to control their behavior and actions. Individuals suffering from OCD unintentionally develop certain habits that become part of their routine. Some habits include washing their hands over and over, repeatedly checking or verifying that things are a certain way, and continuously experiencing negative or obtrusive thoughts.

• Post-Traumatic Stress Disorder (PTSD) is caused by a traumatic event in a person's life. A particular memory or flashback associated with the event can trigger a panic attack. People with PTSD display heightened irritability and emotional or physical outbursts when undergoing a panic attack. Drug abuse and depression are common problems of people living with PTSD.

All the above types of anxiety are listed based on their intensity. Anxiety varies from mild to severe and has different effects on each person. As mentioned before, anxiety is an entirely natural behavior that all human beings experience and is sometimes necessary to help identify potential danger. It only becomes dangerous and harmful when it crosses a limit and becomes symptomatic. If you believe that you are experiencing symptoms of anxiety, it is recommended that you seek professional help.

Chapter 2:
How Anxiety Starts in a Relationship

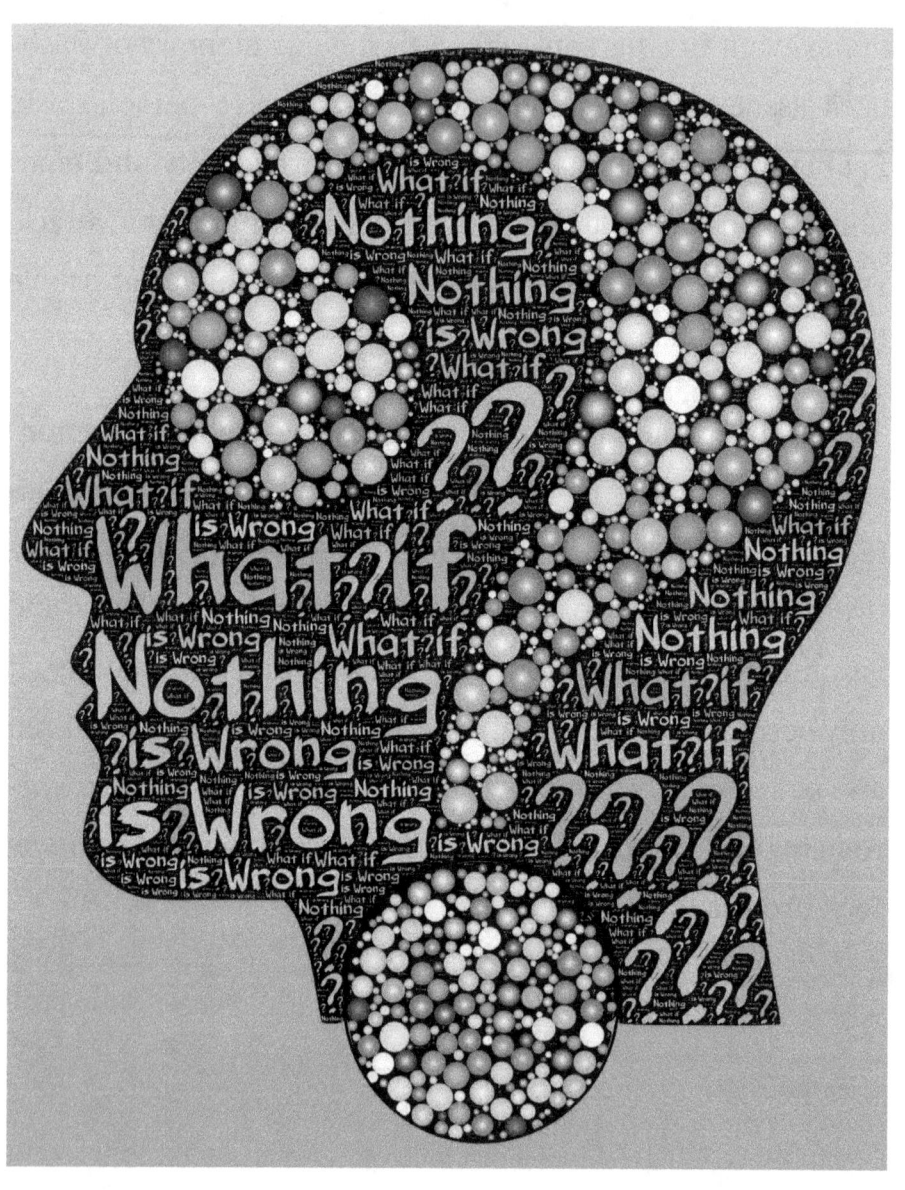

Nobody wants to lose their connections with family, friends, and loved ones. Still, the sad thing is that this sometimes happens without us knowing the reasons why. There will always be ups and downs, rude or unkind behaviors, financial problems, work or school pressures, and many other problems in any relationship. We all have different life experiences and go through different mental states throughout the day. Some of these experiences are painful or even traumatic. They can lead to emotional outbursts or unhealthy behaviors that can drive the people around us away. When these behaviors become a regular part of your interactions with your loved ones, they can begin to have a potentially permanent effect on your relationships.

Suppose your partner has never experienced a mental illness. In that case, it can be difficult for them to understand what you're going through.

For example, depression and anxiety often make the person withdraw from social life and their loved ones, which might be very difficult for their significant other to comprehend.

Obsessive thoughts and tendencies are also symptoms of anxiety disorders. It's human nature to want to give and receive love and affection. However, some people can become overly possessive over people and things, which leads to feelings of jealousy and insecurity. When they aren't getting the desired love and attention from their loved ones, they start feeling anxious. They can also experience anxiety or panic attacks when they think they're being avoided or neglected. This is one of the most common causes of anxiety in relationships.

Excessive attachment to a romantic partner is also indicative of an anxiety disorder. Thoughts of separation or not getting the desired attention and responses from their partner can profoundly affect people who suffer from anxiety disorders. A psychotherapist can offer tips to help you be a grounding, supportive presence for your loved one if something triggers an attack. Asking what they need from you and providing love, support, and understanding are crucial when helping a loved one through their symptoms of anxiety and fear. However, keep in mind that severe panic attacks should be immediately reported to their treating specialist.

Self-confidence—or lack thereof—is yet another primary reason for anxiety in a relationship. For many people, anxiety comes from low self-esteem and the belief that they aren't "good enough." As such, meeting new people is often an excruciating ordeal. These feelings of insecurity and inferiority can cause severe stress and depression.

However, you must keep in mind that your low self-esteem is only a product of mental illness. Talk-therapy is a fantastic way to learn to overcome your feelings of insecurity and learn true self-love and acceptance.

Do you ever fear that you aren't "good enough" for your significant other? Or that they "deserve better"? Try talking to your significant other about how you feel. Overcoming these issues can be easier with the right care, support, and attention from family and friends, in addition to therapy and medication. Never take your mental health lightly—opening up to the people who love and care about you is the first step to recovery.

A healthy romantic relationship is one that can roll with the punches, handle the ups and downs, and not be destroyed by the inevitable end of the "honeymoon phase."

Many people entering a new relationship talk about that "butterflies in the stomach" feeling when their new love interest so much as walks by. You have probably experienced it yourself. You want this feeling to last forever and for your relationship to be absolutely perfect. You go out of your way to make the best impression, sometimes at the expense of your true feelings. Maybe you start changing some aspects of yourself to fit with your new partner. You begin second-guessing every decision you make.

At the beginning of a relationship, this level of stress is not healthy and can lead to even more serious problems later on.

Here are some things you can do to overcome the stress of starting a new relationship.

First, you have to identify the root cause of your anxiety and your fears of not being the right person for your partner. When you meet someone you like, you will naturally want to develop a relationship with that person. As you continue with your relationship, you might start thinking negatively about yourself. The bad memories may begin to pop up, reminding you of things you're not proud of, making you feel unworthy of love.

All these negative thoughts are unreliable, though. More often than not, they come from your anxiety disorder or depression. You have to face them head-on and not let them rule your life—and ruin your relationship.

If you feel ashamed of something in your past, you'll likely experience the fear that your partner will find out about it. While it's important to keep in mind that you are in no way obligated to share every single aspect of your past with your significant other, sometimes keeping a big secret can be very stressful and ultimately harmful to you and your relationship.

Chapter 3:
Insecurity in relationships, how to overcome it, what are the symptoms, and how to recognize them

I seemed to destroy every romantic relationship in which I had ever been involved. Not because of infidelity, nor because of incompatibility. Not even because of fights, boredom, or need for personal space. They were all destroyed because of a trance-like state that would consume my entire being on an extremely regular basis. Almost as if I were possessed by a demonic entity. I would become hypervigilant, as observant as a private investigator. I would become a quick and intensely sharp manipulator. Warm anxiety imbrued energy would rapidly swell up from my feet to my stomach, all the way up my throat. I would lose control of my thoughts and words. All of these symptoms were seemingly caused by my obsession with my partner's past. I would bombard my partners with personal questions about their previous relationships. No stone would be left unturned, and the obsessions would fester for days, weeks, months, and years at a time. A myriad of imaginary images and thoughts of my partner's past would be cycling through my mind minute after minute with no respite. When I finally went to sleep, I would suffer an onslaught of nightmares, watching these re-imagined past encounters of my partner play out like a movie. In waking, I would name, blame and call my partner all kinds of derogatory names. I wasn't consciously aware enough to control the outward assault on the world and the people around me.

What Are the Symptoms of Insecurity and How to Recognize Them?

Blaming

If you are always reprimanding or blaming your partner for everything, you need a rude awakening. This happens when your ego is controlling your relationship and utilizing manipulative tactics to do it. Do you ever assume responsibility for the things that you do? Would you be able to take a step back from the situation and think from another perspective without accusing the other person? The ego will want you to find fault and scrutinize for others' mistakes. It will do everything and anything to transfer blame and criticize another person. Shockingly, that thing we evade is generally what we end up receiving in our relationships. If you fail to take responsibility for yourself, your ego will help you project everything onto your partner.

Playing the Victim

Is it safe to say that you are playing the unfortunate victim card in your relationship? Do you always compare yourself with your partner? Is it true that you are continually putting yourself down? An unhealthy ego will help you reinforce negative actions as opposed to positive ones. It will cause you to focus too much on your imperfections. It is unquestionably time to venture back and conduct a recheck on your relationship if you are doing this. You are not a saint.

The time has come to be responsible for what you are bringing to the table and stop constantly blaming your partner for everything.

Being Jealous

Jealousy is the green-eyed monster, and it usually sets the stage for negative drama in a relationship. The ego tends to feed on self-esteem and the absence of acknowledgment. A cherishing relationship depends on the regard and consciousness of each other. Love doesn't contribute to comparing, putting down, and criticizing as ego does. This is a show that turns into the most astounding type of negative drama in any relationship. If you are in an abusive relationship, your ego won't let you leave because of jealousy. What is making you consider these ideas? Does your partner make you question the validity of your relationship? This means you need to venture back and be straightforward about identifying the abuse in the relationship.

Fearing Rejection

This kind of dread prevents you from proceeding onward and accomplishing any of your goals. When you stop yourself as a result of this dread, you are unfair to your relationship. Changing the way you perceive things as opposed to being incapacitated by the anxiety and uneasiness caused by your ego will be a healthy way to increase self-esteem. Negative self-talk will only feed your ego. Don't compromise on who you truly are to surrender to your partner's ego. This is anything but healthy. A loving relationship depends on mutual respect and acknowledgment. On the off chance that you are feeling rejected, maybe it's time to re-evaluate your relationship.

Always Having the Last Word

Your ego has a way of making every little thing about you and turning it into a one-person play. If you find that you talk a lot about yourself and don't ask about your partner, well, you are immensely ego-driven. The ego assumes a superb role in shielding us from accomplishing total harmony and joy. It is the mind's method for controlling. It will likewise create situations in your mind that don't exist. If you find that you need to have the last say in all things, it's time you venture back and discover the root of this need. Do you feel like you are better than others or second rate? Do you lack self-confidence and, in this manner, need to demonstrate that you are worthy despite all the trouble? The ego will make you conceal your sense of mediocrity by overhyping yourself. If you and your partner fight a lot, your ego probably fuels these fights. Is this how you feel important in your relationship?

It is important to take a step back and observe your relationship at times. You need to identify when you are the one in the wrong and making mistakes. Take a look at your actions and acknowledge when they are driven by ego. You have to let go of your ego if you want a strong, healthy relationship with your partner.

So if you have a big ego or your love is egotistical, what should you do?

For the narcissist, being correct all the time is deeply connected with their sense of self-worth. In this way, the individuals who can't relinquish their egos do and say anything they want and always think they are correct. Tragically, this will be at the expense of a lot of other things. Their need to always be correct can cost them their relationship with colleagues, supervisors, relatives, and, more often than not, their partners. Sooner or later, you have to understand that the bogus self-esteem you get from adhering to your ego and "being correct" doesn't exceed genuine happiness.

Being true to yourself and practicing mindfulness will enable you to understand that you can't be right in every circumstance. There will be certain situations where you make a mistake, have a wrong mentality, or are essentially on the wrong side.

It may be hard to admit this at times; however, having the ability to concede when you're wrong can be quite liberating. Assume responsibility for your actions and decisions, and you will soon see that the ball will be in your court!

Understand that you don't have to be better than everybody else either. The need to be this way can be quite destructive for you. A great sense of ego leads you to believe that you are superior to every other person. It is similar to remembering that you don't need to be correct constantly. That is not a healthy level of competitiveness in anyone.

There will always be somebody better, prettier, more astute, quicker, and wealthier than you. No matter how old you are, this will always be the way of things. The sooner you understand that you cannot—and ought not to feel committed to—be superior to other people, the sooner you can repair and improve your relationships.

Rather than contending with others along these lines, why not consider improving yourself? You are perfectly unique. Focus on how you can improve yourself, and every one of your relationships will take a turn for the better.

Exercise: it is imperative to see how activity impacts the body as well as the mind too. Daily exercise is essential in an individual's life. When you exercise regularly, your brain discharges endorphins into your circulatory system, improving your mindset. Besides, your psyche will be occupied for restless musings. Exercising has been deduced to help your general state of mind and decrease the indications of nervousness and sadness. As physical exercise increases, so relieves your anxiety. A few activities to take an interest in that have been explicitly connected to assisting with tension are yoga and judo. This is because these activities help individuals be careful in their development and center themselves spiritually while clearing their brains. As you structure an everyday practice with your activity, your body will start to deliver serotonin and endorphins during and after exercise. These synthetic concoctions that are provided in the brain appear to diminish melancholy and uneasiness fundamentally. Training supports confidence, improves certainty, enables you to start to feel engaged and reliable, and causes you to manufacture substantial and new social connections and companionship.

Begin a healthy diet: the brain requires an enormous measure of vitality and sustenance to work effectively. Healthy nutrition can bring enormous changes in your physical health. A terrible eating regimen implies that you are not providing the required supplements for your brain's synapses to work effectively. In light of that, it might be worsening the manifestations of your nervousness. By following a sound eating regimen and filling your plate with entire and new nourishment, drinking the perfect measure of water, and guaranteeing that you are taking in the correct nutrients, minerals, and Trans Fats day by day, you are giving your cerebrum the proper nourishment to battle anxiety. A solid eating routine likewise implies dealing with your guts and stomach related tract. Recollect that a sound eating routine removes improved beverages like frosted teas, soft drinks, and prepared natural product juices. Studies have demonstrated that individuals who drink an over-the-top measure of pop each day are over 30% bound to experience the ill effects of nervousness and melancholy than those who don't. Unsweetened beverages like plain espresso, homegrown teas, and water that has organic products in it are far more beneficial alternatives when keeping your body and cerebrum hydrated. Caffeine is likewise a supporter of tension side effects and ought to be curtailed to battle caffeine symptoms.

No more liquor: liquor is a focal sensory system depressant and is a known reason for tension, and we all know that it is very harmful to our health. A few people do attempt to dull the impacts of their nervousness by drinking liquor; however, actually, liquor is regularly the base of your tension.

Liquor intrudes on rest, dehydrates the body, and occupies an individual from managing the current issues as opposed to going up against and recognizing the root and reason for their anxiety.

Catch up on your rest: bad dozing propensities affect an individual's state of mind. This is because the brain's synapses need time to rest and recharge to keep the body's mindset steady. Legitimate long rests enable the cerebrum to adjust hormone levels and allow an individual to all the more be likely to adapt to their anxiety. If plagued with unhealthy sleep patterns and sleep deprivation, you needn't bother with synthetic compounds to be amended. Awful resting propensities can be rectified utilizing natural remedies and techniques, including melatonin, teas, homegrown mixes, exercise, and contemplation. When you ensure that you are getting high-quality rest and your mind will start to address its hormone levels.

Begin to address your feelings: this book covers dealing with your negative contemplations and frames of mind broadly. Being restless manipulates the brain into creating more hormonal concoctions to attempt to feel upbeat. In the end, the cerebrum gets exhausted and can't deliver the correct dosage of hormones required to keep your system healthy, happy, and tension-free. Via preparing your psyche to consider reflection emphatically and care thoroughly, you can change your recognition of what's going on and start to assume responsibility for your negative considerations. By battling and hushing your negative contemplations, you can work through your nervousness, ensuring you are better ready to recuperate in your relationship. Make sure to rehearse all types of positive confirmation, which incorporates excusing yourself, appreciating your life, and showing consideration to other people. When you can get positive, uneasiness begins to slow, and you are better ready to speak with your accomplice without negative, foolish conduct subverting you. Keep in mind that you are responsible for your life. If there are circumstances that are making you tense, you can transform them.

Reduce your pressure: stress builds nervousness higher than anything and triggers the body's battle or flight reaction. By learning techniques to manage pressure and control and focusing on factors, you enable your body to all the more likely deal with its normal reactions to what it sees as a risk. Distinguishing what makes worry for you enables you to either remove the pressure or create methodologies to help you deal with it. Rehearsing unwinding systems, setting aside effort for yourself to revive, and appreciating life are large approaches to loosen up your mind and enable nervousness to ease. Become flexible to stress and realize that, by and by, you have power over pressure.

Reach out and locate a solid help base: a stable relationship begins with solid fellowships. Having a decent informal organization that offers you support and a sounding board as you work through your tension is critical to mending. Uneasiness can make an individual need to detach themselves; however, a decent help structure implies you will consistently have somebody to connect with when tension rears its head. These ought to be individuals who locate the positive things in you and can give you sensible and objective reactions when you talk about what is causing your uneasiness. They should provoke you to investigate inside and should assist you with quieting your inward pundit. Ensure that you keep in constant contact with your loved ones who make you like and love yourself. Do whatever it takes not to become involved with others' pessimism. Attempt to volunteer to increase your perspective in life and associate with others who have emotional wellness issues. On the off chance that you are not yet at the point where you need to see an advisor, attempt to join a care group. Consider adopting and caring for a pet to help soothe your nervousness and show you unconditional love.

Find your motivation: people who have a definite feeling of their motivation can better deal with pressure and nervousness than those who don't. Finding your inspiration gives you a boundary against the impediments your internal pundit outlines for you. Those with a solid feeling of direction will, in general, find life to be all the more satisfying and can see the positive qualities in each circumstance instead of stressing over what terrible events may occur. Your motivation doesn't need to be a vocation or a leisure activity. Finding your otherworldliness, investing energy considering your qualities, volunteering at covers or no benefit associations, recognizing and utilizing your one-of-a-kind gifts to help other people, and recognizing that life is about rhythmic movement are, for the most part, methods for finding your motivation. When you discover your motivation, you can get strong and fair with yourself, enabling you to be straightforward with your accomplice.

Chapter 4:
Self-Evaluation of Anxiety in a Relationship

How do you know you are anxious in a relationship? What are the signs that show that you are having a negative emotion concerning your relationship? What are the effects of anxiety on your relationship? All of these questions will be answered when you carry out what is called a self-evaluation of relationship anxiety. This chapter focuses on the self-evaluation of tension in a relationship. The essence of this is to evaluate the issue to put an end to it.

Anxiety can spring out at any time in a relationship. The fact is that everyone is vulnerable to this problem; the tendency to become anxious in a relationship increases as the bond becomes stronger. So, there is a need for everyone to carry out a self-evaluation.

Do you spend most of your time worrying about things that could go wrong in your relationship? Do you doubt if your partner really loves you? A sure sign of relationship anxiety is when you become worried all the time as a result of these and similar questions running through your mind.

For proper self-evaluation of this problem, you need to know the signs that show that you are already becoming anxious. Also, you need to weigh the cause and effect of this problem on your relationship. As I have said earlier, the purpose of evaluating is to address the issue before it develops. This chapter is structured to give you maximum benefit, and I will try to be as explicit as possible.

How to Know if You Are Getting Anxious in a Relationship

You might be neck-deep in relationship anxiety without really knowing, so this section will point out the symptoms of this problem to you. If you notice any of the signs mentioned below, you will benefit greatly from the self-evaluation process.

When you feel jealous of your partner

Take a cursory look at your behavior. Do you feel like breaking somebody's head when your partner develops any form of a platonic relationship with the opposite sex? Are you threatened by any friends of theirs you fear may "steal" your partner away from you? This is jealousy, and it is one of the signs that you are feeling anxious in your relationship. Sometimes, you might even have the urge to test your spouse's commitment and love; this indicates anxiety triggered by jealousy.

When your self-esteem is low

When you are always cautious of how you behave because you don't know what your partner's reaction will be, or you can't express yourself freely in front of your partner due to fear of rejection, this is an indication of low self-esteem - a sign that you are anxious in your relationship.

Lack of trust

Your partner is one of the people you should trust the most. If you always have to confirm whatever your wife, husband, boyfriend, or girlfriend says before you believe them, it shows a lack of trust in the relationship. Many times, the lack of trust is caused by past betrayal. However, you should not allow past betrayals to negatively impact your relationship, provided they were one time occurrences. Realize that your partner is not perfect, and once they have assured you that such incidences will never happen again, believe them.

Emotional imbalance

Today you are frustrated, tomorrow you are angry; the next day, you are happy – this is emotional instability. You might not be aware of this, but constant mood swings are also signs of emotional imbalance, and they do not help the matter.

They only worsen it. Whatever problems or issues you are facing, discuss them with your partner. When the two of you deliberate on a problem, you will get it solved quickly. When you discover that your mood is not stable, it is a symptom of anxiety in a relationship.

Lack of sleep and reduced sex drive

The aftermath of constant worry is insomnia, which is the inability to sleep, and when you are unable to sleep, your body is stressed, leading to decreased libido.

If you are experiencing one or more of these symptoms, you need to figure out the possible causes and deal with them. I am going to give you examples of likely causes of these problems.

Possible Causes of a Relationship Anxiety

Most times, relationship anxiety could be a manifestation of a deep-rooted problem. Here are the common causes of relationship anxiety:

Complicated Relationship

When you are uncertain about your relationship, or it is not clearly defined, it can be classified as complicated. This applies to those that are dating. For instance, a woman may not know the man's intentions - whether he wants to marry her or is just in it for fun. Also, a long-distance relationship could result in anxiety. In such cases, partners must learn to trust each other.

Comparison

Comparing your current relationship with past ones should be avoided as much as possible. You might begin to entertain feelings of regret if you discover that your previous relationship was better in the areas of finance, communication, sex, and other aspects. To avoid this feeling, you should never compare your marriage or relationship to that of others or those you have had in the past.

Constant fighting

When you are always quarreling with your partner, you might never stop worrying because you don't know when the next altercation will crop up. This is one of the causes of severe anxiety in a relationship because your bid to avoid quarreling will not allow you to have a pleasant time with your partner.

Lack of understanding

Partners that do not take the time to understand each other will always face difficulties. As mentioned earlier, the constant quarreling will result in an anxious relationship. Are you noticing the symptoms of anxiety coupled with miscommunications? Lack of understanding might be the reason for your relationship anxiety. Get to know your partner better, and encourage them to know you.

Other issues

Difficult experiences in past unhealthy relationships might result in many other issues. Not only that, neglect during childhood, abuse in the past, and lack of affection are reasons why someone can feel anxious in a relationship.

Once you have identified the root cause of your relationship issue, getting rid of it will be the next step. Do not forget that the primary reason for the self-evaluation of any problem is getting rid of it.

Effects of Anxiety on Relationships and How to stop it

This section will examine the effect of anxiety on a relationship with logical steps towards ending it and how anxiety manifests in a relationship. The effective ways to stop it, no matter the way it appears, will also be highlighted.

Anxiety makes you continuously worry about your relationship

Persistent worry is one of the manifestations of relationship anxiety. If you are continually having thoughts such as, "Is my partner mad at me?" "Are they pretending to happy with me?" or "Will this relationship last?" These kinds of views indicate one thing – WORRY. If you discover that you regularly entertain these kinds of thought, do the following:

- Clear your mind and live in the moment.

- If negatives thoughts are continually running through your mind, then stop, clear your mind, and think about the beautiful moments you have shared with your partner. Think about the promises your partner has made, and reassure yourself that your relationship will stand the test of time.

- Do not react impulsively - think before you take any step. Share your feelings with your partner rather than withdrawing from them - make an effort to connect.

Anxiety breeds mistrust

Anxiety makes you think negatively about your partner. You will find it difficult to believe anything they say. In some cases, you may suspect that your partner is going out with another person. These kinds of feelings inevitably come between you and your partner. It makes it hard for you to relate to them well. To put an end to this, follow these practical steps:

- Ask yourself, "Do I have any proof of my suspicion?"

- Go to your partner and talk things over with them.

- Start again if you notice that your relationship is suffering from a lack of trust.

- Reestablish the trust, date each other as if it is your first time, and gradually build the trust.

- Do the things you did when you first met each other.

Anxiety leads to self-centeredness

What anxiety does is take all your attention, making you focus solely on the problem while every other thing suffers. You don't have time for your partner; you are withdrawn into yourself. You focus mainly on yourself and neglect the physical and emotional needs of your partner. Here are the things to do to get rid of this attitude:

- Rather than magnifying and focusing on your fear, pay attention to your needs.

- You can seek your partner's support when you discover that you cannot handle the fear alone.

Anxiety inhibits expression with your partner

Anything that stops you from expressing your sincere feeling to your partner is an enemy of your relationship. Anxiety is the culprit here; it hinders you from opening your mind to your partner. You think that they might rebuff you or that telling them how you feel may cause an adverse reaction from them. This makes you keep procrastinating instead of discussing the critical issues right away with them. How do you overcome the fear of rejection? Consider the following quick steps:

- Focus on the love your partner has for you.
- Voice out what you feel to get rid of anxiety.
- Approach your partner cheerfully.
- Discuss heartily with them

Anxiety makes you sad

Anxiety breeds these two problems – limitation and fear. A soul battling with these two evils cannot be happy. Anxiety is that culprit that steals your joy by preoccupying you with unnecessary agitation and worry. Happiness is the bedrock of any relationship, so stop being sad and start enjoying happy moments with your partner by taking the following steps:

- Dismiss any thoughts that make you sad.
- Play your favorite music to occupy your mind.
- Become playful with your partner.
- Relive the sweet moments you have had with your partner.
- Be humorous, laugh with your partner.

Anxiety can either make you distant or clingy.

One way by which you can recognize anxious people is that they tend to be extreme in their actions. If they are not aloof, they will become too attached. Both of these behaviors are extreme and unhealthy. Have you evaluated yourself and discovered that you are guilty of these extremities? Take the action steps below to restore your healthy relationship with your partner:

- Figure out your feelings.

- Work on yourself.

- Get yourself engaged with things you enjoy doing.

Anxiety makes you reject things that will benefit you.

It makes you see everything from one point of view - fear. Anxiety results in indecision in a relationship because you won't know which way is right. Here is how you can stop this problem:

- Acknowledge your confusing thoughts and deal with them.

- Weigh your decisions carefully without being biased.

- Seek your partner's help if you discover you need support.

Chapter 5:
Practical Strategies to Solving Anxiety Issues in a Relationship

Partners/couples generally face challenges that need to be addressed as the partnership progresses. Your ability to manage issues as they come up in your relationship will ultimately determine the relationship's growth. If a challenge is not well managed, you may find your relationship in a crisis and may need to take concrete steps towards charting a way out.

Some of the challenges that most people face in their relationships include communication, joint development as a couple, relationship needs, contentedness and autonomy of the partners, equal rights, routine, habit, sexuality, loyalty, stress, quarrels, conflicts, difference in value systems, distance, illness, and the list goes on.

How careful are you in your relationship? Being careful and considerate of each other saves a lot of frustration in the relationship. Do you live in the here and now? Can you enjoy the moment? Living in the here and now sounds easier than it is. More often than not, our thoughts slide into the past or the future.

Other questions to ask yourself about your relationship:

How intensely are you enjoying the moment? Does your partner always understand what you mean? Do you have common interests with your partner? Do you find relish in sharing in each other's lives and experiences? Are both of you a well-rehearsed team in all walks of life? Do you find security, tenderness, and sexual satisfaction with your partner? How about division of labor - does it work well between the both of you? Do you find peace, support, and security in your relationship? Can you talk about everything very openly? Does your partner make you strong and happy?

The answers to these questions will guide you into a proper self-evaluation of the challenges you might be facing in your relationship.

In most cases, men do not like relationship talks. Nevertheless, it is necessary to have regular discussions about needs and wishes in a partnership. Especially for conflict resolution, communication strategies are needed. Firstly, you must distinguish between generally communicating as partners and communication as a result of conflict resolution. Communication about each partner's wishes, ideas, plans, and hopes is an important foundation for a relationship. Couples who are happy in long term relationships are usually able to communicate their feelings to each other. They do not see themselves or their relationship threatened by these expressions, even if they are negative without being aware of it. They can develop their own very subtle language, gestures, and facial expressions throughout their relationship.

Quarrels are normal in a relationship - it is "how they arise" that matters. Clashes arise when you or your partner are strained by external stress. For example, a job, problems in raising children, conflicts in the family, etc. The stressed partner often communicates in a more irritated and violent tone.

It is in our greatest interest to be proactive and inventive regarding how we communicate with those closest to us.

Creating, maintaining, and nurturing relationships with friends, co-workers, and family, not just partners, is critical for our well-being.

Rather than looking to others to create relationship changes, the simplest place to start out is with yourself.

A Relationship Self-Assessment

Below is a list of some relationship statements. Go through the statements and note any that don't seem to apply to you. Write these down on a separate sheet of paper.

1. I have told my spouse/partner/children that I really like them within the previous few days or weeks.

2. I get on well with my siblings.

3. I get on well with my co-workers and/or clients.

4. I get on well with my manager and/or employees.

5. There is nobody I might dread or feel uncomfortable running across.

6. I place relationships first and results second.

7. I have forsaken all of the relationships that drag me down or injury me

8. I have communicated or tried to speak with everybody I may have hurt, injured, or seriously disturbed, though it may not have been 100% my fault.

9. I don't gossip to or about others.

10. I have a circle of friends and/or family who I love and appreciate.

11. I tell people close to me that I appreciate them.

12. I am completely wrapped up in letters, emails, and calls relating to work.

13. I always tell the truth, even if it may hurt.

14. I receive enough love from people around me to feel appreciated.

15. I have forgiven those people that have hurt or broken me, whether or not it was deliberate.

16. I keep my word; people can rely on me.

17. I quickly clear up miscommunications and misunderstandings after they occur.

18. I live life on my terms, not by the principles or preferences of others.

19. There is nothing unresolved with my past lovers or spouses.

20. I am in tune with my needs and desires and ensure they are taken care of.

21. I don't judge or criticize others.

22. I have a supporter or lover.

23. I talk openly about issues instead of grumbling.

Chapter 6:
How to Help Your Partner If They Suffer from Relationship Anxiety

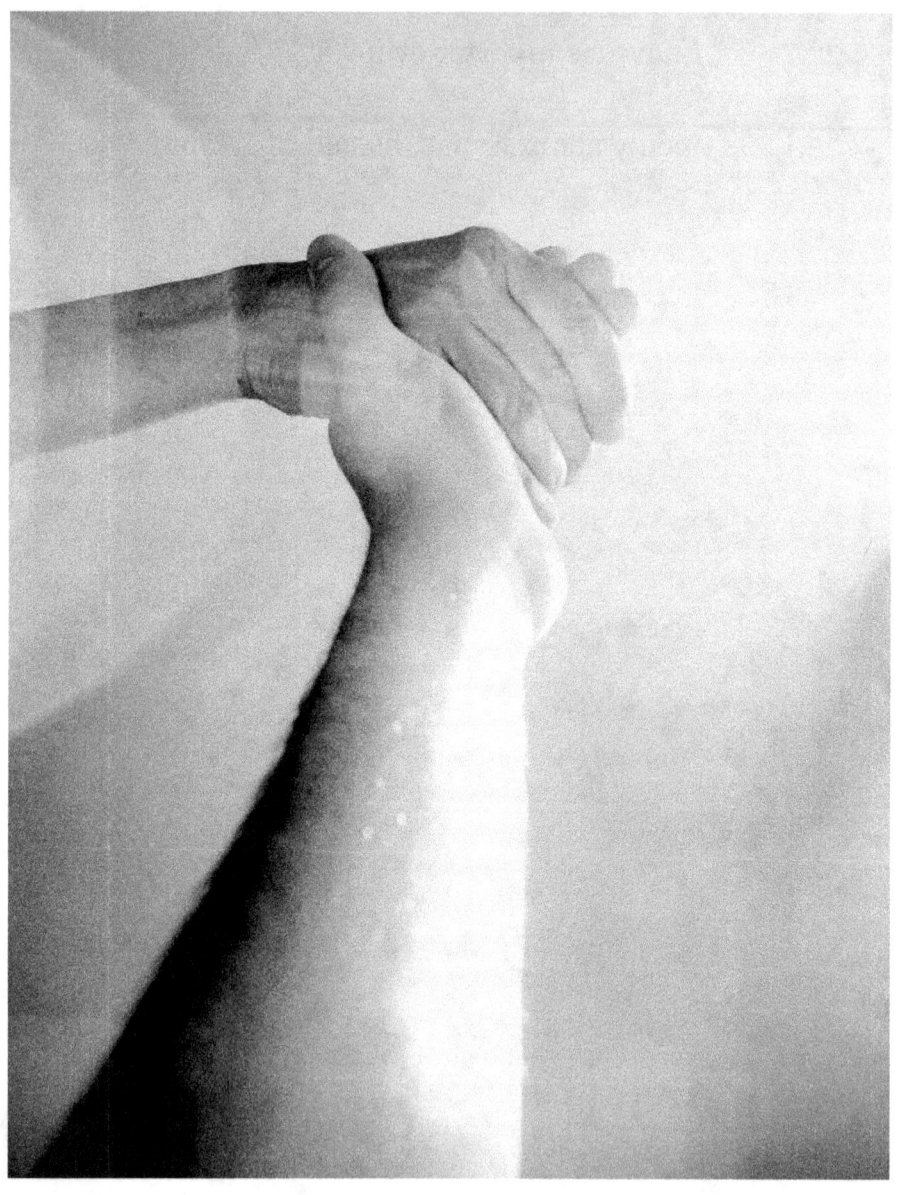

Relationships and love demand that we get involved in our partner's life, which means we always have to be supportive and loving. If you have a partner with one or more types of anxiety, you are already aware of how it can influence not just the relationship but also your life. You should know how to recognize the signs and learn how to neutralize an anxiety attack by relying on previous experience.

Your involvement in your partner's journey of learning how to live a life free of anxiety is of great importance. When it comes to sudden panic attacks, you can do several different things to help distract your partner and ease any suffering. When it comes to chronic anxiety, you are the one who will get involved in exposure therapy. There are specific strategies you can take into consideration when it comes to each type of anxiety. This part will help you recognize which kind of stress your partner is struggling with and learn how to help him. You will improve and enhance your relationship's quality, strengthen the bond you have, and confirm your love and devotion to your partner.

Acute Anxiety

Acute anxiety happens out of the blue. It can be caused by different things, specific situations, or other people you and your partner meet. It occurs suddenly, and there is no time for planning and taking it slow. You need to be able to react in the moment and to know how to assess the situation. Understand what is happening, what your partner is going through, and come up with the right way to neutralize the anxiety. There are four ways you can take to be supportive and helpful in case of acute anxiety:

Be calm, be compassionate. If you are not, you won't support your partner's needs in that moment. If you give in to anger, frustration, or anxiety, it won't help. It can even make things worse. You also need to remember not to give in to your partner's anxiety and accommodate it. In the long run, this is not helpful. Instead, offer understanding, not just solutions.

Assess your partner's anxiety. What level is it? What are the symptoms and signs of an anxiety attack? An anxiety attack can hit with a different strength each time. You need to recognize it to choose actions appropriate to the given situation.

Remind your partner of the techniques that helped with previous anxiety attacks. Whether it is breathing or exercise, your partner is probably aware of their success in neutralizing anxiety. But in the given situation, maybe they need reminding. Once they are on the right path to dealing with anxiety, your job is to provide positive reinforcement. Give praise and be empathetic once your partner executes techniques that will help with the attack.

Evaluate the situation. Is your partner's anxiety attack passing? If it is, be supportive and encourage your partner to continue whatever they are doing to lower their anxiety. If it stays at the same level or increases, you should start the steps from the beginning and develop different techniques and strategies to help your partner with an acute anxiety attack.

Chronic Anxiety

To address chronic anxiety, you might have to try out exposure therapy, as it is considered the golden standard of treatment by many people. Usually, it takes the guidance of a professional therapist to try exposure therapy. But, if the level of your partner's anxiety is not severe, you might feel comfortable enough to try it on your own. In this case, you have to guide and learn how to be a supportive person for your partner.

Exposure therapy works by creating situations that trigger your partner's anxiety. It will help your partner learn how to tolerate certain levels of anxiety. Your partner will learn how to reduce anxiety and how to manage it in given situations. Over time, you might get surprised at how your partner now partakes and enjoys situations that previously made them anxious.

You have to start with the least challenging situation and progress slowly and steadily towards more challenging ones. Don't push your partner to the next level until they are ready. If anxiety isn't decreasing in the first challenge, it's not time to go to the second. If a situation is causing too much anxiety, and your partner feels they are not ready to deal with it, go back to the previous challenge, and work on it again.

For example, let's say your partner has a fear of heights. They want to overcome this fear and be able to climb the building's last floor. How will exposure therapy look in this case? Tell your partner to look out the window from the ground floor for precisely one minute.

Climb to the second floor together with your partner. Remember that you are not just an exposure therapy guide; you also need to support them. Make them look out the window from the second floor for one minute. In case of anxiety showing up in its first symptoms, remind your partner to do breathing exercises to reduce its impact.

Once your partner feels better, they should try looking out the window again.

If no anxiety presents itself, you should leave your partner's side. They need to be able to look through the same window, but this time without you.

Climb to the third floor and repeat steps three and four. When your partner feels ready, continue to the fourth floor, sixth, and so on. If your partner's anxiety is too high, don't hesitate to stop. The first session doesn't need to take longer than 30 minutes.

Each new session needs to begin with the last comfortable floor your partner experienced. You don't need to always start from the ground floor, as your partner progresses, feeling no anxiety when looking through the window of the second, third, even fourth floor.

Take time. Your partner will not be free of the fear in just a few days. Be patient and continue practicing exposure therapy in this way until your partner can achieve the goal and climb the last floor.

The goal of exposure therapy is not just to get rid of fear and anxiety. It should also teach your partner that discomfort can be controlled and tolerated. Your partner will have an opportunity to practice anxiety-reduction techniques in a safe and controlled environment, with you playing the supporting role.

Plan for Relieving your Partner's Anxiety

Now you know potential techniques you can use to reduce your partner's anxiety. Use this knowledge to create a plan, make a list of practical actions and ineffective actions when your partner experiences an anxiety attack. It is important to remember what to do in situations that trigger anxiety, but it is also essential to know what not to do.

You and your partner might disagree with what is helpful on the list you are making. It is because your partner craves for accommodative behaviors you express when they are under an anxiety attack. Remember that these behaviors relieve anxiety, but in the long run, they do more damage. Try to explain this to your partner. You need to make them understand why such behavior is not suitable for anyone.

Teamwork is beneficial when it comes to fighting a partner's anxiety. But your partner might not want your help due to feelings of shame or thoughts of not needing help. Try making a list on your own. It's worthwhile to do what you can to elevate your partner's anxiety.

The "What-Works" List

When making a list of things you can do to help your partner with anxiety, it is essential to communicate effectively. Be specific; question your partner how does it make them feel when you perform particular tasks. How does it feel when you join in breathing exercises? Depending on the personality and level of anxiety, they might even want to be left alone. Maybe they need to be reminded during the panic attack to take short breaths and then perform this task alone.

Choose the right intervention for particular symptoms. Learn to recognize your partner's needs in time and offer help.

Here is an example of an anxiety relief list:

- If I am nervously pacing the room and unable to relax, offer to go outside for a walk with me, or suggest taking a walk out alone.

- If I am complaining about work without pause, distract me by choosing a movie we can watch together or suggesting a book I can read alone.

- **If I'm obsessing over whether I turned off the iron, reassure me I did and remind me that not repeatedly checking is one step closer to recovering from my OCD.**

During a panic attack, fast and shallow breathing helps. Remind me how to perform it and join me in this task.

The "What-Doesn't-Work" List

When we love our partner, we feel we will do anything to help him or her. In our efforts to help, we might not realize that we are doing more harm than good. We do mean well, but we don't have the experience, patience, or knowledge of what is happening to our partner during an anxiety attack.

Sometimes even our partner reinforces us to perform tasks that are bad for his anxiety in the long run.

It may look complicated, but both you and your partner need to be honest about behaviors that help alleviate anxiety. It will take time and patience to practice to avoid specific actions that bring relief. Here is an example of a "what-doesn't-work" list:

- I will never again tell my loved one, "just get over it."

- I won't manipulate my partner's feelings to make them stop this behavior.

- I won't use drugs or alcohol to get over my partner's behaviors.

- I won't disrespect my partner's phobias and mock them.

- I won't reinforce my partner's anxiety by accommodating the behavior.

Having a list of what to do and what not to do when anxiety gets triggered will help you and your partner be more in command of your lives. It will stop you from making your partner's anxiety even worse, and it will put both of you on the right track to overcoming the anxiety. Your relationship will become vibrant, more satisfying, and fulfilling. Anxiety cannot be defeated just by taking the steps on the list. They are just things to do to help your partner overcome fear at that point. You will need to take more severe measures to overcome anxiety fully.

A professional therapist will be of great help. It may take some time to find the right therapist for your partner, and it will take some persistence. Therapists may fit one type of personality but not the other. Be sure your partner is paired with the right therapist, and that will help. Encourage and support your partner, and in time you will learn how to manage their anxiety and possibly even watch them completely overcome it.

Chapter 7:
What is jealousy, how to overcome it, what are the symptoms, and how to build trust in the relationship

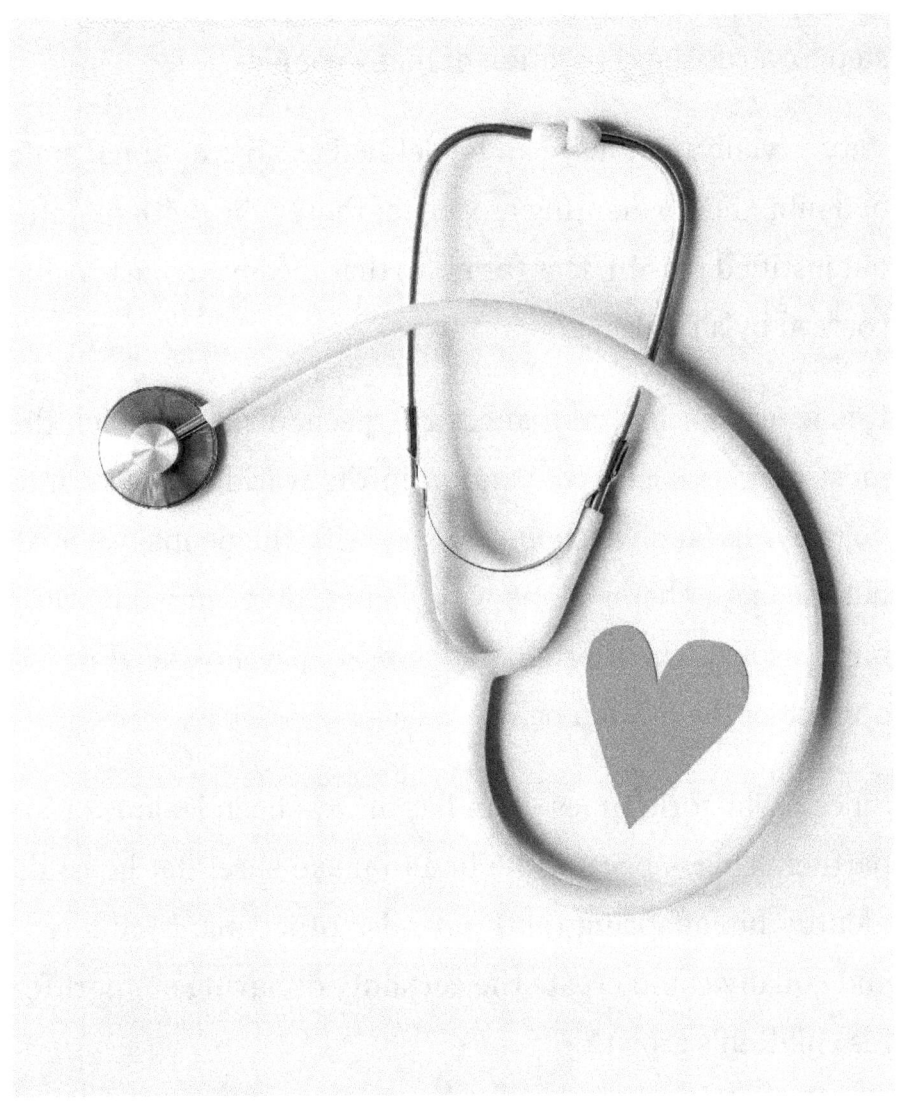

It is evident to everyone that there is a relationship between love and jealousy, even if this connection is hardly clear: on the one hand, there are those who believe that the jealous lover keeps the couple's intimacy alive and protects it. It is well known that being jealous is often the first step towards the separation of many couples.

Very trivially, jealousy can be defined as an emotional state of doubt and tormenting anxiety of those who, with or without justified reason, fear (or note) that the loved one is being coerced by a rival.

It is a very ancient and ancestral mechanism on which the most famous social convention in the world is based: monogamy. In fact, we choose to stay with the people we love, but the fact of being alone with them is determined by various reasons, which originate from the psycho-social development of the human being.

Since prehistoric times, man has always been jealous of his partner. This is because he had to make sure that he could identify his offspring (and not raise other man's children) and equally could create the certainty of having support for his children's growth.

If initially, this feeling had nothing to do with love, with time and the advent of modern culture, the belief that jealousy and love are somehow connected has grown stronger and stronger, until arriving to affirm that without jealousy, there is no love.

But is it true that you cannot love if you are not jealous? And if so, how much and how should we be jealous?

"Healthy" Jealousy

It could be said that jealousy is the fear of losing what we care about, and, in the case of relationships, this concept is identified with the fear that the loved one stops wanting us and prefers anyone else to us.

If we want to prevent this person from leaving our life, we should not be indifferent to signs (real or alleged) that they begin to snub our attention or ignore us to devote their time to others.

At this point, the issue of limits arises.

Above what level is jealousy "acceptable" and useful for properly preserving a relationship, and when does it become harmful and destructive?

It could be said that this depends on the role we play in the relationship and on how the subject that threatens us (real or imaginary) tries to insinuate itself into this relational space.

For example, suppose a man sees another man courting his wife. In that case, it is right and healthy for the relationship that this situation generates a certain level of jealousy in him, precisely because his role in the exclusive relationship with his partner is threatened.

Every lasting relationship contains many feelings, experiences, and a wealth of mutual knowledge that the two partners must dutifully defend to not lose their identity as a couple.

This is why a suitor, or worse, a lover, can tear a relationship to pieces even before they have succeeded in their intent: ousting the partner from their role is often enough to undermine the balance of the couple.

Romantic Jealousy

Jealousy of someone you love and fear losing is called romantic jealousy in literature. The dynamic of romantic jealousy develops in a triangle made up of three fundamental elements: 'The Self' (the jealous person), 'the Loved One,' and 'the Rival.'

The dynamics of amorous jealousy and its constituents:

1. The belief that some relationships are configured as objects of possession and give the right to request or prohibit certain behaviors (even to prohibit, paradoxically, feelings and desires);

2. The fear that 'the Rival' will or may undermine the possession and enjoyment of 'the Loved One,' causing partial or complete loss;

3. The prediction that if this were to happen, the jealous person would have damage (suffering from the loss of the object of love or its exclusivity) and a bruised self-esteem.

This type of jealousy is characterized by a strong feeling of possessiveness towards the loved one and, therefore, by believing that you have the right to prohibit or impose certain behaviors on your partner. However, sometimes one can also be jealous of almost unknown people, which excludes the absolute presence in the dynamic of jealousy of possessiveness. In relationships, there is sometimes the fear of losing the loved one because of the rival. This fear is present even if, in reality, the real threat of a third wheel in the couple relationship is completely absent.

Another important element in this type of jealousy would be the expectation of possible harm if the loved one were to betray; that damage would lead to a strong loss of self-esteem. Therefore, it is easy to understand how situations that cause jealousy can have real foundations but can also be caused by unfounded fears projected by the jealous person within the relationship or by minor behaviors that simply overshadow the risk or suspicion of infidelity. As for 'the Rival,' some authors point out that the most feared rival is the one who possesses the positive characteristics that approach one's ideal self, rather than the ideal of the loved one.

Is Hunger for Love, Anxiety, and Depression Related?

Love, with its sweet seductions, false truths, and atrocious acts of revenge, has been walking alongside us since we were children, and thanks to it, we are born, we grow up, we feed ourselves, and, sometimes, we poison ourselves.

Is love, hunger for love, anxiety, and mood deflection interrelated?

Apparently disjoint, they seem three elements without any connection between them, but in reality, they are closely connected and intersected with each other.

We know well that the ability to choose a partner first and being a couple afterward depends on how we have been loved and, more importantly if we have been loved.

Childhood, Autonomy, Dependence, and Love

The early experiences of care nourish the soul and self-esteem and then contribute to transforming that child, in need of care and love, into an independent adult, serene and capable of relating to their partner and the world, without that child's atavistic wound often carried around if they are "not loved."

The "wound of the unloved" is often the cause of a lack of basic trust and love if it affects our partners and the bond of love.

The partner is not chosen only based on physical and personal attraction, but on the basis of a lot of other things, often "invisible to the eye."

Many love stories are stories between accomplices and childhoods - or childhood chasms - alike.

The choices of love are often "collusive choices." Many times the chosen partners are those who, in some way, lead back to the land of childhood.

The hunger for love, closely related to the "wound of the unloved" - that atavistic lack of love, like an indelible mark, moves the ranks of affective and relational choices - are closely related to anxiety and the deflection of the tone of the mood.

Couples, Love, and Separation Anxiety

Working steadily with couples, shipwrecked, unresolved, separating or separated, I can say that the health of the couple and their quality of life depends on the health of each protagonist of that bond, from how and if they were loved, and from the ability they have to give within the bond of love.

- Anxiety by separation

Another element of central importance is separation anxiety.

When one of the two, or both the protagonists of that love, is moved by crazy jealousy, by an impetuous need to control the other, and by the fear - almost terror - of losing the partner, there are all the elements to shipwreck - sooner or later - that bond.

It is, in fact, a "hungry, needy, dependent love," a bond in which victim and executioner alternate, nourishing and keeping alive the emotional dependence.

In 'Fragments of a Love Discourse,' Roland Barthes wrote in a very suggestive way: "I hurt the other."

Some Symptoms of the Hunger for Love

The hunger for love almost always manifests itself with the same characteristics, atrocious and unbearable:

- An unbridgeable need for love
- A sadness dreadful to bear
- Love seen and experienced as an aid
- Hyper investment by the partner

- A despairing dedication to the beloved

- Savage jealousy

- Possessiveness

- Need for confirmation and certainty

- Anxiety and separation anxiety

- Never feeling loved enough

- Lack of interest in oneself and one's own interests (with an emotional shift towards the partner)

- Extreme devotion

- Anxiety and panic in the face of any mishap or temporary distance from the partner

- The total absence of borders with the partner, tendency toward symbiosis, and a fusional relationship

The protagonists of these sick loves are often unresolved on the psychic level and are trying to find the cure for the soul's ailments in love and a relationship.

So, can anxiety and depression be the cause and consequence of the hunger for love?

In those suffering from addiction, love becomes a drug, a real psycho/physical necessity, to the point of transforming itself into the joy and pain of their own life.

They are crazy loves.

Unhealthy Love

Love, inhabited by excesses, imbalances, lack of balance.

These loves are loves characterized by a massive desire, never completely satisfied, of absolute and fusional love - always and in any case nourished by abandonment anxieties - often moved by the need for confirmation from the other.

Symptoms of Anxiety and Mood Deflection

When love brings suffering with it, sooner or later, the body begins to complain, to cry out that something is wrong, and that love will tend to be wrecked.

The body, as we know, expresses itself with the language of symptoms which, in reality, are the gateway to the soul:

- Various aches and pains, sine causa

- Psycho-motor agitation
- Endless sleepless nights counting sheep
- Disorders of the oral-alimentary sphere
- Tachycardia.
- Palpitations, the strange and annoying sensation of feeling the heart
- Pain in the center of the chest
- Pressure drops
- The terrifying feeling of having lost control over one's body, and one's destiny
- Breathing difficulties and a feeling of suffocation
- Increased urinary frequency
- Disorders of the menstrual cycle
- Sexual response disorders: anorgasmia and sexual desire disorders
- Diffuse and somatic anxiety

- Irritability, inability to unplug

- Ease of crying, poor modulation of emotions

In summary, our body is the litmus test of our soul and our psycho / physical well-being or malaise.

Listening to it, taking care of it, and having the ability to understand if a Love is a love that nourishes or impoverishes, cares for, or destabilizes, is the quickest way to happiness, or at least, serenity.

Chapter 8:
How to eliminate negative thinking and the fear of abandonment

In addressing negative thoughts, various approaches can help. The good news is that this manual will shed light on the best ways to deal with your ideas to prevent it from graduating to anxiety disorder.

One meaningful and helpful way is to make mental shifts. In other words, intentionally adjusting the way you think of challenging an established thought pattern. This happens by changing the way you judge an event or situation. It is a form of training for the brain such that it doesn't succumb to anxiety generating thoughts.

This will not be a straightforward process because it involves "uninstalling" and "deprogramming" many negative behaviors and thinking patterns responsible for anxiety. For instance, if, as a little girl, your dad kept hammering that no one will love you if you are fat, you end up being haunted by that for life. Hence, you might even resort to unhelpful means to try and keep fit.

Beware of thoughts that place excessive demands on you. They start with "I" or "should." Many a time, these demands are impossible to live up to, which ends up fueling our anxiety. Consider the following:

Instead of...	Try...
I should wake up early tomorrow.	I will sleep early and try to wake up early tomorrow.
I should stop eating this kind of food.	These food items are not healthy for me. I need to be in good health; hence taking... will help.
I should make more friends.	I need to go out more often, make myself approachable, and smile, hoping someone will notice and talk to me.

The problem with this sort of thought is the compulsion and pressure it puts on us. When this gets to an unbearable level, we end up procrastinating or avoiding what we want to do as a means of escaping. In the long run, this ends up triggering more anxiety.

With this in mind, rather than telling yourself you should do things, think of a kind, calm and gentle approach to keep yourself motivated towards the task before you. You can think of another means without graduating into a negative thought pattern.

How to Control Negative Thoughts to Beat Anxiety.

The good news is that you can take many positive steps to have a turnaround and break free of the cycle of thoughts that causes anxiety. You can come up with a viable strategy to counter those thoughts to prevent anxiety. This section explores how you can control negative thoughts:

Turn Negative to Positive Action

Should you be bewildered by an obsessive thought that's calling you to do something, listen to the dictate of that thought and attend to it. In the same way, you will not ignore the check engine light of your vehicle forever. No matter how hard you try to avoid looking at it, it is right before you every time you are driving. You will not, because of the check engine light, discard the vehicle or give it out. In the same manner, should thought be a cry for help, do not ignore it.

In other words, take a break and attend to the situation. If you feel scared and tense to the extent of triggering anxiety, take a break and consider what is making you afraid. Rather than pushing the feeling away, take some time off, examine why you are scared, and look for how to address it.

Once you are calm enough to deal with the matter, come up with an action plan. By this, I mean positive and actionable steps that can help. Doing this should address the real source of the anxiety rather than push the thoughts away.

Avoid Indulging in the Level of Futility

In dealing with unhelpful thoughts, there is a tendency to keep doing what doesn't work. However, the problem is evident – they never work. The issue is how easy it is easy for the brain to succumb to these useless tactics repeatedly.

With this in mind, rather than falling back to self-defeating thoughts, consider another approach. It is not about fighting old habits but noticing what doesn't work and sticking to what does.

Expand Your Awareness

A constricted mind is like a tight muscle. The degree of movement will be minimal. A few of the things that constrict the mind are old beliefs, inertia, habits, fear, low expectations, and old conditioning. You, however, need to confront this with all honesty.

A closed mindset does no good. With this in mind, on detecting any inner discomfort, be sure to expand your awareness. For instance, a feeling of hatred towards your neighbor is a clear example of a contracted mindset. However, with an open mindset, you can tolerate the person and see another good side of them rather than seek out their fault.

Combat Shades of Green Thinking

Our mind has been conditioned to taking the easy way out. In thinking and making decisions, we love the easy way as it speeds our progress and helps our decision making. This is about dealing with black and white thinking patterns, which could be challenging as it holds the person to irrational beliefs.

Rather than getting anxious with shades of gray thought, I recommend evaluating circumstances on a scale of 0 to 10. Falling short of expectations should be seen as a partial failure, rather than sinking into anxiety and beating yourself up.

For instance, someone could say, "I am very useless; I could not wake up to go over my notes for this evening's exam." However, how sure are you that missing a single morning will affect your chance of success? When you analyze this on a scale, it could be a 7% likelihood. This helps removes the anxiety of looking at the circumstance in terms of complete failure.

See Disappointments as Part of Life

You might not be able to do much about disappointments. With this in mind, condition your mind to expect them once in a while. Avoid overthinking people and circumstances so that when things go in a way you didn't anticipate, the blow will not be too much. Life will throw a lot at you. Bear in mind that your reactions to all the happenings have a lot to do with your well-being. You can either sink into anxiety or rise above it, seeing it as part of life.

It is vital to know the difference between the things you can control and the ones you cannot. It takes a wise man to let go of things he cannot control. This is the secret to happiness and rising above anxiety that comes with disappointments. You were jilted despite your faithfulness and dedication to the relationship. It hurts, I know, but mourn it and move forward, preparing yourself for the next available partner.

Challenging Unhelpful Thoughts

Our thoughts and the way we give in to thinking can affect our anxiety levels. Most of these thoughts take place outside our control and are often hostile and irrelevant. We should always remember that these are mere thoughts; they have no solid basis and are not always facts.

Although it is straightforward to believe most of our irrelevant thoughts when we are anxious, we should also remember that they are often wrong assumptions, most times figments of our imaginations, and need to be questioned.

Fear of Abandonment

Fear of abandonment is the overriding fear that people will leave near you.

Everyone can develop a fear of giving up. It can be deeply rooted in your traumatic experience as a child or in adult depression.

When you fear failure, maintaining healthy relationships can be almost impossible. The paralyzing fear will drive you away to avoid being harmed. Or you may be sabotaging partnerships unintentionally.

The first step to overcoming anxiety is to understand why you feel like that. You can address your fears on your own or through therapy. However, fear of abandonment may also be part of a personality disorder requiring treatment.

Different Types of Fear of Abandonment

You may fear that someone you love will physically leave and not come back. You might be afraid someone will give up your emotional needs. You can either maintain yourself in ties with a parent, partner, or friend. Examples of abandonment fear:

Fear of Emotional Abandonment

It may be less noticeable, but it is no less painful.

Emotional needs exist for us all. In case these conditions are not met, you may feel unrecognized, unloved, and disconnected. You may feel very much alone, even if you are in a relationship with a physically present person.

If you have undergone emotional renunciation in the past, especially as a child, you may always be afraid that it will happen again.

Fear of Abandonment in Children

It is normal for babies and children to experience a period of separation fear.

They may scream, yell or refuse to let go if a parent or caregiver is leaving. At this stage, children have difficulty understanding when or if the person will return.

As they begin to understand that they come back, they resolve their terror. This happens to most children by their 3rd birthday.

Abandonment Anxiety In relationships

You can actually be afraid of allowing yourself to be insecure in a relationship. You may have problems of confidence and worry about your relationship too much. That can make your partner suspicious.

Over time, the anxieties will cause the other person to retreat and keep the cycle going.

Symptoms of The Fears of Abandonment

When you fear abandonment, you can likely identify some of these symptoms and signs:

- Too sensitive to criticism

- Trouble trusting in others

- Difficulty making friends unless you are sure you want them

- Take extreme measures to prevent rejections or separation

- Pattern of unhealthy relationships

- Staying in a relationship even at the point that it is not healthy for you

- Blaming yourself when things don't work

- Trouble committing into a relationship

- Working too hard to please people

- Getting attached to people quickly and moving on quickly

Causes of Abandonment

Abandonment problems in relationships may be due to having been emotionally or physically abandoned in the past.

For example:

- As an infant, a parent or caregiver may have died or just up and left.

- Parental negligence may have been felt.

- Your colleagues might have rejected you.

- You have been through a loved one's chronic illness.

- A romantic partner may have suddenly left you or acted untruthfully.

These events can lead to a fear of abandonment.

Long-Term Effects of Fear of Abandonment

The long-term effects of the fear of giving up may include:

- Challenging connections with friends and romantic partners

- Poor self-esteem

- Issues with self-confidence

- Mood swings

- Codependence

- Depression

- Fear of intimacy

- Panic problems

Examples of the Fear of abandonment

Here are a few examples of what the fear of giving up may look like:

Longer-term effects of fear of abandonment, you may think, "No connection, no drop."

- You are obsessively worried about your perceived flaws and what others might think about you.

- You are the most pleasant people. You don't want to take any opportunity that someone doesn't like you to stay there.

- You are crushed when someone criticizes you a little or gets upset in any way.

- When you feel slighted, you overreact

- You feel insufficient and unattractive.

- You split with a romantic partner so that they can't break up with you.

- Even if the other person asks for space, you are clingy.

- You are often jealous, suspicious of your partner, or critical of him.

Fear of abandonment is not a diagnosed mental health disorder, but it can be detected and discussed. Fear of rejection may also be part of a diagnosable personality or another condition to be treated.

Recovery Problems

Once you know that you fear loss, you can do some things to start recovery.

Remove some slackness and stop the harsh judgment on yourself. Mind all the positive qualities that make you the right partner and mate.

Speak to the other person about how this fear came to be. But be aware of what you deserve from others. Explain where you come from, but don't make up something to fix your fear of abandonment. Don't expect more than is fair from them.

Work to maintain friendships and build a support network. Strong friendships will strengthen your sense of belonging and self-worth.

If this is not practical, consider talking to a qualified therapist. You will benefit from individual advice.

How to Assist Someone with Abandonment Problems

Some strategies you can try if someone you know has to deal with the fear of abandonment:

- Begin the conversation. Encourage them to speak, but don't press.

- Understand that the fear is real for them, whether it makes sense or not.

- Make sure you're not going to abandon them.

- Ask what you can do to assist.

- Suggest treatment but don't push it. If you want to start, offer your help in finding a professional therapist.

See your healthcare provider for guidance if you have attempted but cannot manage your fear of self-abandonment or if you have signs of panic disorder, anxiety disorder, or depression.

You should continue a full check-up with your primary care physician. You can then consult a doctor to diagnose and treat the illness.

Personality disorders can lead to depression, substance use, and social isolation without treatment.

Fear of abandonment will affect your relationships negatively. But you can do things to minimize these fears.

If the fear of dropping out is part of a broader personality disorder, drugs and psychotherapy can successfully treat it.

Chapter 9:
How to resolve conflicts and save your relationship (especially in marriage)

It's quick to miss one aspect in today's world of television dating shows, mobile applications, and romantic comedies: relationships are work. They need time and commitment. We never "swipe correctly," fall in love, and live happily ever after. And when things get rough, it's easy to throw in the towel, suggest, "it wouldn't have worked out anyway," and step on – rather than do the work to learn how to maintain a relationship.

But it's worth protecting your relationship.

You've got a past. You've been through a lot together – a lot of relationships over the last few years or even decades before you came to this stage. Your partner loves you better than anybody else, so they're going to be there for you when no one else would. Before you give up all hope, seek these nine ideas about how to save your relationship.

1. *Examine your focus*

Conflict is dangerous as you concentrate on protecting yourself against assault rather than on solving the issue. It's because people's minds will be focused on avoiding "hitting the pole," in other words, not confronting problems because they believe they have an out-clause. But our attention is on our course. If we don't want to hit the pole, we need to focus on what we want to do: stay on the road! We may change the result by shifting our emphasis.

This lesson is on how to save your relationship. When you focus on where you don't want the relationship to stop, struggle, and allow frustration to build-up, you'll find yourself where you don't want to be — either in a miserable, unfulfilling relationship or totally apart from the spouse. If you work on dispute management and evolve together, you'll get the results you expect.

2. *Communicate*

Two couples were faced with a dispute – the same problem, in reality. But one of them understood how to settle a dispute in a relationship, and the other did not. One responded by depending on bad behaviors and using the disagreement to enlarge the distance between them. The other used confrontation as a way to express their emotions and grow their relationship. What couple do you think has the most positive, satisfying relationship? What kind of relationship do you think would last longer? Communication is at the top of the list of ways to preserve a relationship.

3. Turn conflict into opportunity

Don't get defensive; don't pound your point; don't attempt to fight: one couple has learned these ways to settle a dispute in their relationship. Do you still want to sacrifice your partner, the one you love? If you agree that there are no losers in life, you will let go of small disagreements and indulge in good conversation.

Conflicts are ways for you and your partner to match beliefs and consequences. They are likely to recognize, respect, and accept disparities. Put yourself in your partner's position and seek to grasp his or her understanding. Such experiences and emotions may be painful, but we will never develop if we only want comfort.

Conflict is also a way to know more about your partner and to respect them more intensely. Begin to see disagreement as a step to something new, rather than as a cause to withdraw. The next time you find yourself disagreeing with your spouse and contemplating how to save your relationship, remember to see the best in the scenario rather than the bad, and consciously trying to work together towards a more stable future.

4. Use humor

If you're in a retaliatory loop, a strong strategy is to use comedy to interrupt the trend. Humor will relieve stress and enable you and your partner to concentrate on what you really want – discovering how to sustain the relationship – rather than on what you just don't want, another meaningless fight. If you notice the argument is worsening, take a minute to stop it. Try talking to Christopher Walken or William Shatner. Singing a song that makes your partner laugh. Render the tension too absurd.

Few spouses would have transformed the scenario into a dispute, but by using comedy to nip the cycle of retribution in the bud, you and your partner can seize the moment and converted it into an opportunity to practice how to resolve the conflict in the relationship.

5. Ask the right questions

If you're considering how to save a relationship, it's possible that things have been going bad for quite some time. Not only do you need to reach into the background to discover the specific, deeper problems, but you need to look to the future. It's just about asking the correct questions about yourself.

Second, make sure you continue this exercise with the best mind. The point is not to criticize, dig up old arguments, or remind your partner of all the stuff they're doing that annoys you. You will shift your attitude to one of appreciation and approval. Take note of the reality that life is going on for your partner, not just for you. Even your relationship's present condition offers you an opportunity to improve and develop – as long as you remain responsive to what it has to teach you.

Now you're brave enough to ask yourself the most critical questions: Why did your relationship break down? Are these the restricting values that have influenced the relationship between you and the partner? How are you going to conquer them? What do you like about the future? What's the relationship going to depend on?

6. Practice acceptance

Apply your new open-mindedness to your partner. Our partners do somethings or have behaviors that annoy us because no human being is perfect. Instead of focusing on their derogatory attributes or poor behavior, concentrate on what they bring to the table, how they make you look, and the things you enjoy. You will notice that you will quickly begin to enjoy all the things that used to make you mad, as they are part of the whole person, your partner, whom you love.

Respond to your partner, consider what they think and why they act the way they do it. And understand yourself, too: be frank with your own thoughts and emotions. Be thy own self. Human shortcomings aren't meant to be the explanation of why you're wondering how to save your relationship. Basically, they're a great tool to show your partner how much you value them.

7. Be aware of your negative patterns

Conflict with your spouse can make you feel assaulted or endangered, helpless and fragile, which may make you panic and retreat. When something that your spouse does annoy you, and you feel like you're under attack, you're less inclined to react constructively, so you're more apt to return to old standbys like "the silent treatment" that can eventually do more damage than good. Eventually, that would lead the relationship to break down entirely.

If anyone asked you if you know how to settle a dispute, you would undoubtedly say yes, and if they asked you if passive treatment was a good approach to cope with the issue, you would almost definitely answer no. You know better than to succumb to these dumb tactics, but if you're upset enough, you do it anyway. Why? Why? Why fall back on destructive habits instead of actively trying to correct the relationship problems at hand?

Break the cycle of aggression and offer constructive energies to the dispute. Don't take the defensive; don't pound the point; don't try to defend. How would you want to sacrifice your partner, the one you love?

8. Work on forgiveness

When you're considering how to save your relationship when your confidence has fallen, you're likely to feel furious, frustrated, wounded, and mistrustful, and a variety of other negative emotions. When you're the one who broke the trust, you feel bad and ashamed. You may also seek to condemn your partner or defend your acts. All spouses need to focus on reconciliation in this case.

You're not only going to wake up every day and feel good about forgiving your partner. Forgiveness is a form of process. It's a collection of little actions – admitting faults, exercising total integrity, and placing your partner first – that adds up over time. Forgiveness is taking a role.

If you broke your partner's trust, you would have to take complete responsibility. Be mindful of how badly you upset your partner, and give them the support they deserve. Place the partner first so you don't slip into a trap of self-denial. If your faith is lost, take some space, but keep communicating. Let your spouse realize what you need to restore your trust. Most of all, never give up on that.

9. *Make time for touch*

When you're always fighting with your partner — when every little thing they do bothers you — it can be hard to be affectionate. But you've got to make time for touch. It doesn't only mean sex – it also means cuddling on the sofa during a movie, stealing a morning kiss before work, and holding hands for no reason at all.

There's a reason why loving your partner helps you feel so good: cuddling, kissing, and even rubbing your hands, triggers the production of oxytocin, a "feel-good" hormone in your brain lets you feel protected and secure. Oxytocin will reduce pain, help you relax, make you feel more connected to your partner, and also reduce your blood pressure. You get all the advantages of getting over and taking your partner's hand.

Don't deny physical affection – except when you're upset – otherwise, you may find yourself in a totally sexless relationship or marriage. If you really want to learn how to save your relationship, continue with your physical contact. Cuddling until bedtime. Keep your hands while you're out for dinner with your friends. Sneak in a hug when you're enjoying dinner. Physical affection is not the product of a good relationship – it produces a happier relationship. Relationships aren't that simple. We are all people, and human beings make mistakes. We've got weaknesses. Sometimes, we just don't get into the work that we need to do, and we just let our relationships fall by the wayside. When we start looking at ways to save a relationship, it may have been ignored for years. But note this: a lot of relationships are worth preserving. You also need to be able to do some sort of work.

Conclusion

It is important to take care of yourself while in a relationship because you are not only responsible for your own well-being but the well-being of your partner. Remember that there are resources out there just waiting to help you get through this tough time. It is a process, but there are ways to get better. Everything will be okay!

Love is enjoyable when you let go of the anxiety that comes between you and your partner. When you give anxiety a chance to run free in your love life, it may be difficult to know when and how to react to sensitive situations. This may lead you to feel indifferent or unconcerned to some vital relationship issues or put on a show of being uninvolved and forceful when speaking with your partner. While it's certainly not your fault, it's beneficial to understand how anxiety may be affecting how you see things.

When it feels like anxiety is genuinely keeping you down, you will need to overcome it both for your well-being and your relationship's health. By putting all the tips and techniques learned from this book into action, you will be able to overcome every anxiety and insecurity in your relationship. The strategies in this book aim to help you learn positive adapting attitudes to managing your anxiety in the right manner. That can mean having a more advantageous relationship by maintaining a strategic distance from certain anxiety-related errors.

Anxiety is love's most noteworthy executioner. It makes others feel as if you are suffocating them. It's not easy to overcome this, but it's possible.

Anxiety makes it hard to realize what's important and what's not. It can blow things out of proportion, distract us, and cripple us. But it doesn't have to control us.

You deserve to be in a happy, loving relationship that isn't marred by anxiety's vicious grip. All it takes is a conscious effort and a new perspective to realize that anxiety's weakness is a loving connection. By strengthening your relationship, you weaken anxiety's grasp. What's a better example of a win-win than that?

Questions for Couples

Amazing Questions to Build Emotional Intimacy in Your Relationship

Introduction

Couples seek advice from other couples. And while there are plenty of books out there that provide you with useful insight on how to answer this or that issue, how does one go about finding the right questions to ask?

By "right questions to ask" I am not referring to questions that will get you deep into the mind of your partner, although such questions are useful. Rather, I am referring to questions that help you get a clear sense of how your partner thinks about important things in life and what their attitudes are. In other words, questions that can help you better understand your partner's views during the early stages of relationship formation.

You see, though couples often come together initially due to some physical or emotional attraction they feel with each other (perhaps because they share similar backgrounds or because one or both of possesses social prowess), it is not only these qualities that make or break a relationship in the long run. Rather, it is how well the partners understand and deal with each other's attitudes and beliefs that determines the fate of the relationship.

In fact, one of the most important aspects of successful relationships is the ability to connect over topics considered important by each partner. Couples who share similar views about these "core" topics are more likely to stay together over time, whereas couples whose views are incompatible tend to live unhappy lives and eventually break up.

The purpose of this book, therefore, is to help you better identify your partner's "core" topics by focusing on questions that will get you thinking about these very issues. Of course, the specific questions you ask will depend upon your partner and what your relationship is like at the present moment. So in addition to suggestions for general conversation topics, you will also find specific questions for use when discussing each one.

Finally, you will find some recommendations on how to identify a topic as core by paying attention to how your partner reacts when certain topics are discussed around them.

For example, if your partner shows an intense interest in a particular issue that tends to upset them (such as if they cry during an argument over said issue), chances are that this issue is core to their life and that of their immediate family.

These discussions can be quite difficult and may leave you or your partner feeling a bit uneasy. Don't worry. It's worth it! In fact, this process is essential if you ever want to have a healthy relationship.

Couples who have a hard time talking to each other without getting upset, or those who have trouble communicating in general (often in stressful situations) may find some of the issues discussed below helpful. They can be considered core to the lives of most people, and therefore they will have an important impact on your relationships with loved ones. This does not mean that just because you think one or more of these questions are relevant you should ignore any other areas that trouble you and your partner – it is still important to find out where your spouse is coming from on all matters. But it does mean that if you're having trouble communicating with your partner, then these questions can be a good starting point for useful discussion.

This book is a compilation of questions on many topics related to how couples live their lives. Some are broader and some are more specific, but most will help you to talk with your partner about how you feel and think. Some of these questions have been around for years, while others were inspired by recent events in modern psychology research and literature. The point is that all of them have been selected because they make people think, and that's the key to a good conversation.

This book can provide useful insights in various situations: when you're picking up your partner at the airport, when you're shopping with your wife or husband, or even while sitting down with your kids at dinner. You could even use these questions for talking with friends, family members or other loved ones.

Most of these questions will help you to talk about the things that are important in your life. So keep them in mind next time you and your spouse want to have a meaningful conversation. It doesn't matter if one of you wants to talk about work and the kids while the other wants to talk about politics, religion, or philosophy — just start asking questions!

NOTES

Chapter 1:
Questions on Trust

Trust is a vitally important element in any healthy, loving relationship. Being able to trust your partner is the bedrock of the love you share. Without it, it's impossible for either of you to feel secure in your relationship.

But what does it mean to trust someone? To most people, trusting means believing that the other is being truthful and genuine in their actions, thoughts, and feelings - that they have your best interests at heart without an ulterior motive. But, in practice, this can be difficult to assess, especially in the early days of a relationship. And if you're wrong in your assessment and you trust someone who turns out to be untrustworthy, it can be devastating.

If you have difficulties with trust in your relationship and would like to build a greater sense of security and stability between you and your partner, try asking these questions for couples. They are likely to help you explore what it means to trust as well as define what makes you both feel comfortable with each other.

1. Have you ever felt like you shouldn't trust me?

Couples who trust each other have better, more stable relationships. When you trust your partner, you feel secure in the knowledge that they won't hurt you or let you down. And when they know that they're trusted, they feel better about themselves and their relationship with you. So, if you don't trust your partner, it's normal to feel nervous about what they're doing when they're away from you and whether they are faithful.

If that's the case for you, try to work out why – have there been times when your partner has behaved in a way that made you distrust them, or do you just get the feeling that they aren't as committed as you are? Be sure to talk to each other about how much trust matters to both of you and how important it is in a successful relationship.

2. What if my spouse was unfaithful?

This isn't a question about infidelity itself; rather, it's a question about one possible outcome if your partner were to cheat on you. Like many of the questions in this book (and in life), this one comes from "The Five Love Languages" by Dr. Gary Chapman. His theory is that there are five major ways to "speak" and show love to your partner – through words (quality time), acts of service (physical touch), receiving gifts (words of affirmation), quality time, or through physical touch or acts of service. Some people speak in all five languages; others speak only in one, two, three, while some speak only in the one language in which they're fluent.

3. What are the most important things I have to do to build your trust?

This and the following question (what are the most important things you have to do?) come from "For Better or For Worse: the Science of a Good Marriage" by Tara Parker-Pope.

The opposite of trust isn't expectation — it's betrayal. If you can't trust your partner, then all of the expectations in the world won't make a difference. What we want is for couples to have both trust and expectations; this allows them to work together toward common goals, both at home and in their relationship generally. If you want to build trust in your relationship, you need to find out what your partner needs. When it comes to building specific expectations, each of you has different expectations of the other, which can lead to disagreements (or worse) if you don't make a point of discussing them.

What are the most important things I have to do? What are the most important things I have to be? The answers will help you and your partner focus on your highest priorities for improving your relationship and keeping it strong.

Various therapists who work with couples often ask these questions of partners during an initial session.

4. Do you want to know more about my past relationships?

Couples don't have to share their entire past or even their present with each other. If you do feel like being open about things, then this question is a way to ask it gently and indirectly.

You should never force your partner to share things, but if you're talking about it and they seem hesitant, this question and the next provide ways to encourage your partner without being pushy.

5. What are the most important things I have to do to build your trust?

If you really want to build trust, you have to know what your partner needs. If your partner can't tell you what those things are, you need a more direct question like: what happens when my partner doesn't trust me? Those with a history of betrayal will struggle the most with this question because they may need to think about it carefully before they answer. So be patient while they work through their answer – if it's important enough for them to tell you, then it's important enough for you to wait for them.

5. What would help you feel more comfortable when talking about things in our past together?

This is the mirror of the previous question and one way of asking gently that might cause your partner less anxiety when you do choose to talk about past relationships.

If you do talk about your past relationships, and you and your partner are both willing, it's a good idea to keep a positive frame of mind. That means avoiding the past tense as much as possible when talking about interactions with exes. So say, "I love how so-and-so did this during our last encounter," not "I loved how so-and-so did this...(sniff)...last encounter."

7. How can I build my trust in you?

This question comes from "For Better or For Worse: The Science of a Good Marriage" by Tara Parker-Pope.

The opposite of trust isn't expectation — it's betrayal. If you can't trust your partner, then all of the expectations in the world won't make a difference. What we want is for couples to have both trust and expectations; this allows them to work together towards goals, both at home and in their relationship more generally. If you want to build trust in your relationship, you need to find out what your partner needs. When it comes to building specific expectations, each of you has different expectations for the other, which can lead to disagreements (or worse) if you don't make a point of discussing them.

If your partner has trouble trusting because of past relationships, then this question will help them start working through that issue with you and finding a way they can be more at ease taking new risks together.

8. What do you think we should do if we find out that someone is lying?

This question comes from research I conducted at the University of Toronto's Rotman School of Management and Baruch College in New York City. We found that couples with clear rules for what to do if one or both partners lie were more confident in their relationship and felt less distressed.

In fact, these clear rules for handling relationship problems were more important than both how many problems the couples reported and how satisfied they were in their relationships.

This question is a great way to add a little structure to your relationship and get your partner in the habit of working with you to figure out ways you can handle problems and work through conflicts more effectively.

The technique is based on research by Dr. John Gottman, considered the top relationship researcher in the world

9. Would you trust me if I asked a friend or relative to spy on you?

Asking someone to do this would be an act of distrust, so if your partner said yes, that would be a sign of trouble.

When you ask this question, you are thinking about what to do if your partner lies, so the answer is particularly important. Another reason for asking it is that if your partner says "yes" that would be an alarming indication that they do not respect your boundaries and privacy. Even if they say no, it still may mean they lie too much or feel comfortable doing things behind your back without telling you about them. Secrets breed lies and lying breeds secrets. It's a vicious cycle in relationships.

10. How would you feel about me having a close relationship with someone I work with?

Women tend to be more jealous when it comes to their partner having strong relationships with co-workers of the opposite sex, but men are nearly as bothered by opposite-sex friendships as they are by same-sex friendships — either way, they're concerned about losing their partner through a relationship with someone else. If the work environment is a source of stress in the relationship, then this question can help you or your partner work through the issue.

It's important to understand that no one person is the source of all of your happiness. It's okay to have outside friendships – it just needs to be without secrets. If you think about what makes close friends special, it's probably because they listen to you, tell you the truth about yourself and others. They help and support you, and they're always there for you. You want a relationship with someone at work with those same qualities.

These questions will help you and your partner work on trust issues together. This chapter is designed to help you understand what trust means, how to go about building it in your relationship, and how to deal with problems that arise due to or because of a lack of trust.

I've found that these questions work well during couples counseling sessions. I suggest that all of the couples I work with print out this list and discuss the questions together. It's also a good idea to keep answering them and discussing your answers with your partner even after you complete the exercise in counseling.

If you are having trust problems or have been hurt or betrayed by your partner, it's important to understand that trust issues often take time to heal. It's impossible to get over a past betrayal in one conversation. You and your partner need time and space for healing – plus, of course, good communication skills – so you can work through any problems together and come out stronger in the end.

NOTES

Chapter 2:
Questions on Communication

Communication is one of the most important aspects of a healthy friend or family relationship as well as significant other relationships because it fosters understanding between two people who are sharing their lives. But the importance of effective communication in a relationship is often overlooked, especially in the early days when you are caught up in the excitement of being with someone new who seems to understand you like no one ever has.

If you want to enhance your communication with each other and build a stronger sense of emotional intimacy, try asking these questions for couples. These questions are likely to help you explore your feelings about each other as well as enhance your ability to talk honestly and openly about any issues that might be holding you back.

Vital Questions for Couples to Discuss Together

1. What am I going to do about certain areas in our relationship? What are we going to do about them?

2. How should we communicate with each other?

3. What is one thing I need from you but we haven't done yet? That you feel we can't do yet? How can we work on these things together?

4. What is one thing that you as my partner needs from me but I haven't done yet? That you feel I can't do yet? How can we work on those things together?

5. How are you feeling about our relationship right now, right here?

6. What are the most important things you have to do to build trust in our relationship? What happens when we can't trust each other? What happens when trust is broken between us?

7. How is it different when we communicate about positive things versus when we talk about negative things in our relationship? In our lives in general?

8. What is one thing I do to make you feel less comfortable communicating with me and makes you feel less in control of the way we communicate?

9. How are you feeling about our communication right now, right here?

You and your partner need to create a plan for how you'll deal with areas of disagreement or problem behavior. You should agree to decrease your anxiety.

When there is a problem or an issue you see with your partner, have a plan in mind to address it with them. Plan on doing the following:

• Ask yourself if you are really upset. If so, ask yourself why this is upsetting you and what exactly about the situation might be causing it.

• Let yourself feel what comes up for you emotionally at the moment. Let yourself feel your feelings.

• Think about what you are going to do, say, or change in the situation or the way you react to it.

• Take a deep breath and step back from the situation. Rather than being sucked into reacting immediately, take a moment and consider how you might want to respond or act differently.

• Communicate with your partner (without nagging or yelling) in a calm manner about your feelings about the situation or behavior upsetting you. If possible, try to state your feelings in terms of feeling needs: "I felt disappointed when..." vs "You did such-and-such..."

- Communicate with your partner about what you are going to do differently.

- Agree on what you'll both need to do to make things different.

2. Ask how should we communicate with each other?

You and your partner should agree on how you can best communicate with each other, especially when an issue or problem needs addressing. You want communication with your partner to be as effective as possible so it can help you create a good relationship. You don't want communication to cause more trouble or conflict.

You want to the communication to be:

- Respectful

- Honest

- Focused on shared positive goals

- Based on the idea that both of you have good qualities and are trying to be a good people...not just that you have shortcomings.

- Based on the fact that your relationship is not about idealism but grounded in reality. This means it is based on shared interests, shared values, and what makes sense for the relationship. It's okay to have different opinions about some things as long as those differences don't threaten the core values or interests of the relationship: "We may differ about politics, but we can agree to disagree about that one topic without threatening our relationship."

- Based on the importance of the relationship to you and your partner individually. You care about each other and want to do what is best for yourselves and for the relationship. It's easier to focus on positive goals rather than negative ones.

3. What is the one thing that I need from my partner, but they haven't done yet? That they feel they can't do yet? How can we work on this thing together?

You should discuss what it will take for them to be able to create a sense of trust in the areas where you are struggling with trust. This may be about sharing personal information, behaving in certain ways, or in any other area you feel they need to build trust.

What can you do together to help the other person feel comfortable with issues that concern trust? What can you both do together as a couple that will help your partner trust you more? What is one thing that you want so badly that it creates doubt for them about your ability to handle whatever the issue is? (Maybe they don't want to see pictures of your ex, for example, but you don't understand why they would have a problem with it when it's just pictures?)

4. How is it different when we communicate about positive things versus how it is when we talk about negative things in our relationship? In our lives in general?

Again, this is a good question to ask if you are having problems in your relationship. If there are persistent issues that need to be addressed, pay close attention to how you and your partner communicate when talking about them. If you find yourself being harsh or using a lot of judgment, you might be dealing with some anger or resentment. If you find yourself coming across as overly accommodating, you may be suffering from fear and anxiety. If you find yourself avoiding the whole subject, there's a good chance that some anxiety is creeping into the relationship and causing stress.

Now how are you feeling about the relationship right now, right here? This is a more general question that might be helpful for you and your partner to keep returning to in the future. If you're worried about how your partner feels, ask about it! It might seem obvious from their actions (or lack of action), but sometimes we have a hard time articulating how we really feel about something in words.

What else could you bring up if it seems like they aren't doing a good job at communicating? What can you do together to improve this aspect of the relationship?

What are the most important things you have to do to build trust in the relationship? What happens when we can't trust each other? What happens when trust is broken? These questions will help you both understand the core issues of trust for your relationship. They can also give you an idea about what to do together if trust is an issue.

If your relationship seems relatively healthy, but there are still issues of trust here and there, it might be helpful for you and your partner to work on building trust in other aspects of your relationship. Perhaps you need better communication about how you're feeling or perhaps there's something they need to share more often.

This can be a long list, but it will help you both develop a better understanding of the issues that relate to trust. Use this list along with your own ideas about what is most important for you and your partner in order to improve this aspect of your relationship.

If something is an issue, but you don't see it here, feel free to add it. These things aren't to be taken too seriously. This is just meant to be a resource for you and your partner. However, I have seen these issues cause major problems in relationships. If any of these items are a more serious issue, consider working to solve them together.

You'll also want to pay close attention to the terms used to describe everything and everyone in your life. With constant negativity, the words used to label everything can be more black-and-white than need be. There's a good chance that such a relationship will fall prey to a particular kind of cognitive distortion, called, "all-or-nothing thinking."

When it comes to communicating about positive things and your relationship, keep an eye out for biased language. In other words, when you communicate with your partner about positive things, where are you coming from? Are your judgments and evaluations equally as harsh as they would be for negative things?

Looking into your mode of communication can help you spot issues that they may be having with their own communication. Try to inspect what you do and look for ways that your behavior could be affecting your partner's ability to communicate effectively with you. Are there times when you interrupt them? Do they ever feel like they can't express how they're feeling? Are there ways in which your attitude could be interpreted as controlling?

Asking yourself these questions can help you develop a better understanding of some of the factors that might be involved in your partner's inability to communicate freely and openly with you.

Other relevant questions: what is one thing that my partner does to make me feel less comfortable communicating with them? To make me feel less in control of the way we communicate with each other?

There are two sides to every communication, and even the most respectful, open communicators will have their fair share of issues with how they communicate.

Inspect what your partner does and look for ways that their behavior could be affecting your ability to communicate effectively with them. How are you feeling about our communication right now, right here?

In this chapter, we've covered a lot of areas where trust can be built, and issues of trust can occur. You want to consider how your relationship is coming along in terms of the way that you communicate with each other on a daily basis. This is the basis for all of your relationship.

Your answer depends on where you are right now, and it's important to acknowledge that you will have good days and bad days. That's not a problem – all relationships go through ups and downs. Just try to answer these questions as honestly as you can, even if it takes more than one try. You may want to discuss your answers with your partner to extend the conversation.

When thinking about communication in your relationship, pay attention to how you both feel about the way that you communicate with each other on a day-to-day basis. Is there a difference between how you feel about communicating in general and how you feel when you two communicate specifically?

These questions are designed to help you and your partner communicate in an effective way that will build the trust in the relationship. They are also designed to help you both build a better understanding of how each of you impact the other's ability to communicate effectively with each another.

That said, there is a wide variety of communication styles out there, so don't feel boxed into these questions if they don't work for you and your partner.

NOTES

Chapter 3:
Questions on Fun

Fun and playfulness are often overlooked in relationships, especially in the beginning when you're more focused on falling in love and discovering who you are. But it's important to remember that all relationships need to have moments of fun and playfulness to make them strong and healthy, because the love you share is enriched by the joy you have just being together.

If you want to bring more fun into your relationship, try using these questions for couples. They are likely to help you explore what it means for you both to have fun together as well as what makes each of you feel playful around each other.

Use these questions at any point during your relationship they're especially helpful when getting to know each other better. It's important to have fun with each other, so have fun answering these questions!

1) What do you like most about being with me?

This question is a great way to get things started. It helps you focus on the good, which will naturally lead into deeper conversation. The key to having good playfulness in your relationship is having a sense of humor about yourself and each other.

2) What does it feel like when we are enjoying being together?

What actions do you take? What do you say? How do your bodies move? This question will help you focus on physical playfulness in particular, which can be important if you want to have more physicality in the relationship.

3) How do you like to spend time by yourself?

How do you like to spend time with me? It's important to know that the playfulness and fun in your relationship isn't just about making sure each person is happy all the time. It's about acknowledging each person's separate interests, activities, and joys, as well as bringing these things together.

This question helps you understand what brings joy into your own life and makes it a question of sharing that joy with each other. When that happens, it allows you both to be more playful with each other while still maintaining your own individual characteristics. Which leads us nicely to the next question.

4) What do you like best about me?

This question can be a bit more difficult, because you might not always know how to answer it. You might feel like there isn't much to say or that your love for each other is already apparent. But trust me, this question is a great way to bring deeper conversation and fun. Try answering from different perspectives, such as, "What do you appreciate about me?", "What do you find attractive about me?", or "How have I grown as a person?" You may also want to ask each other questions that allow you both to put yourselves in the other's position for a change.

5) When do you feel most playful with me?

This question is a great follow-up to the previous question. It requires that you think about what it feels like when the two of you are being playful together. A lot of people find this question hard, because they don't believe they have been as playful as they could or that their partner doesn't have the same ideas about playfulness as they do. But focus on what does feel fun to you, and try to understand why some it makes you want to be more playful with each other. Then, think about answering this next question...

6) What do you think I might appreciate about being with you?

If you want to see more fun in your relationship, this is an important question to ask. It requires that each person focus on the other person's perspective, allowing for a deeper understanding. If you don't feel like you know how to answer the question, ask your partner what it might feel like being with them. This will give each of you some insight into how the other person feels.

7) What physical activities do we enjoy together? This is a great question if you're trying to bring more physicality into the relationship. Especially if you aren't used to being physical or don't have a lot of shared interests, this question can be a good way to come up with new ideas of things you can do together. Even if you already know what kinds of physical activities the two of you like, answer the question again. This time, think about it from another person's perspective. What would they find fun and exciting about the two of you being physical together?

Now we move on to some questions more focused on the relationship as a whole…

8) How do you feel when we're having fun?

This is an important question because it's important to remember that each relationship is different. Some people don't feel much of anything when they are enjoying themselves, while others feel a lot of emotions. Some people really notice a change in their body, while others don't. Or maybe you really get into the fun and are more playful than normal. This question will help you understand your partners feelings about being happy and having fun together.

Because each relationship is different, each relationship needs to find its own balance of fun and serious talk. If you don't have time for deep discussions every day, that's okay! For some relationships, it might be more important to set aside some time on the weekend for getting to know each other better, while other relationships thrive on constant communication.

Whatever you need to make your relationship work, you can find ways to add playfulness throughout the week. Maybe try to ask a question during a fun moment together!

For some questions, you may need to think about your answers for a while and spend some time together reflecting. If this is the case, feel free to write down your answers and share them with each other later!

It can be hard for us to remember why we fell in love with each other in the first place. And sometimes we get so caught up in day-to-day life that we don't remember to appreciate what makes our relationship special. That's why it's important to take some time to think about these questions and what they mean for you and your partner. If you're constantly communicating with each other, you'll stay connected during the fun and the hard times. And even if things change, it can help to remember why you fell in love in the first place!

After answering these questions about fun and playfulness with each other, take some time to discuss what it was like to answer them. What did you learn about each other? Did one of your answers surprise the other? Did anything you said make you feel differently about each other, or about your relationship?

Now it's time to get playful!

NOTES

Chapter 4:
Questions on Respect

When a man is motivated by a desire for respect, he will often give you everything you ask, no matter how unreasonable it is, and no matter whether you deserve it or not.

Respect is the outward expression of approval; it can be given only by those who have control of some kind over the person who receives it. "Give me respect" means "Make me feel important." To inspire respect in others we must convince them that we are superior to them in some way. But their position in relation to us is not important; what matters is the way they feel about themselves compared with how they think we feel about ourselves.

This is why we respect those who are self-assured and we usually feel contempt for those who have no doubts. In other words, it is not so much their positive qualities that inspire us to give them respect as the absence of negative characteristics.

When people are aware of their weaknesses, they automatically become unsure of themselves. They want to cover up their inadequacies but do not know how to do so. Though they fear the judgment of others, they can never be quite sure what other people really think of them. In this situation there is only one way for them to be accepted, and that is by constantly trying harder than everyone else. There are only 10 questions important for you and your partner to answer regarding respect:

1. What do you think makes you a better person than me?

To answer this question, you must first ask yourself the following what good qualities do I have that my partner does not? What are the things that I would like to change in my partner—the things that prevent him from being as good a person as I would like him to be?

When a person realizes that his partner is more talented or better at something, he feels inadequate and inferior. And when a person feels inferior toward someone else, he will try to develop feelings of jealousy or hostility so strong that they overpower his feeling of inadequacy. But if your partner has something you want and you don't think you can get it by competing, you will feel tremendous resentment rather than jealousy. Resentment is a powerful emotion that can be used to control and dominate others, and it is one of the most dangerous feelings that can develop in a relationship.

Those who ask this question are often not really interested in the good qualities or abilities their partners possess, but instead they are looking for a feeling of security in relation to something they consider a weakness. For example, if your partner is very generous with her time and energy and knows quite a few people, you might worry that she will find someone else who will take up more of her time than you do.

2. If I tried to behave the way you want, what would stop me?

When a person feels guilty, inadequate, or inferior, he usually has a kind of inner barrier that prevents him from acting the way he wants to. This barrier is like a series of self-imposed negative attitudes that give him something to feel guilty about even before he does anything wrong.

For example, an individual who feels guilty when he shows anger will make sure that his partner is never angry at anybody else; but whenever she gets angry with him, she will be expressing mistrust or resentment because he had thought of doing something she would not have wanted him to do.

People use their personal feelings as an excuse for not taking responsibility for themselves and their relationships. They feel that it is not their fault if their partners don't behave the way they want them because they are naturally good people and would never hurt anyone. But in relationships, they allow themselves to get upset even though they know that at any moment they can change their feelings. The idea that they have done something wrong becomes an excuse for getting upset and blaming others for their negative feelings.

3. What makes a man friendlier and more responsible than he actually is?

When people feel guilty or resentful toward someone for some reason, they act friendlier toward him than he deserves. This is called "being nice." While this may seem like it is being friendly to the other person, it is actually something very different. When a person sees someone of the opposite sex who attracts him, he will usually act in a way that indicates attraction. If he is friendly or nice to her, then he will assume that she will feel good about herself and want to be closer to him because she will think she is so desirable. In fact, if a woman feels attracted to a man and wants to be close to him, she will act more attractive toward him as soon as possible.

Women are usually more direct and open about their feelings than men; they don't have as much trouble being open and honest with their partners. This is why men, when they are un-confident and insecure about their attractiveness, will often try to act friendlier or nicer to the women they would like to be close to than is necessary or justified. Men will show off their ability to be friendly and supportive by offering favors that are not really needed, since they don't feel secure that the woman in question would want them for herself.

4. What can I do that will make you feel that my presence raises your status?

People are so used to acting in a certain way around others that they don't realize how others feel about them. Even though your partner might be loyal and loving, she will still see that something is missing in you, such as more money or better looks. If you can think of a way to act that will make her feel that your presence is not only comfortable but actually elevating her own status, then she will be more attracted to you.

5. How does a person who is incompetent and irresponsible act when he wants to make others feel good about themselves?

Even though many people are not in touch with their own feelings, they usually know if their actions make them feel good or bad about themselves. This is why incompetent people often act in ways that make others feel guilty or ashamed.

They do things that cause them to feel good about themselves by making others feel bad. If a man does something wrong, he will try to make others feel responsible. For example, if a man is poor and can't take his wife out on weekends, he may try to convince her that it's unfair for him to have all the responsibility for supporting the family while she doesn't have any at all. He makes himself seem like the victim, and she feels guilty for not being more supportive.

6. How can I improve my relationships with those people who are already friendly toward me?

If you want to improve your relationships with people who are already friendly toward you, then make an effort to be with them more often. People who are already friendly toward you may feel honored if they can be around you, and this would improve the relationship. If you have people in your life that like being around you, see if there is some way that the two of you could become closer.

7. What emotions do I feel towards the persons who are already friendly toward me?

If you have people in your life who are already friendly toward you, look at what emotions you feel toward them. Are you happy they think so highly of you, or do you feel some jealousy that they have a better relationship another person than you do? If you can be honest with yourself about your own feelings, then it will be easier to find ways to fix these relationships by addressing such issues. If you are close to becoming friends with someone and still harbor jealousy or envy toward them, it will be hard to make your relationship solid because you will always feel like they have something you don't. This isn't the way a good friendship should be, and it's better to address your feelings head on.

If there are people who dislike you, do not immediately assume that they have valid reasons. Someone who dislikes you might simply resent something about your personality. Sometimes people try to improve themselves by learning about how other people behave.

7. How can I be a better person if my friends try to make me feel that I can improve my status?

If your friends were to try to make you feel that you have improved your status by making a lot of money, getting published, or achieving something important, then it is possible that you will change in the way they want. But if your friends are honest and accept you as you are, there is no way that they will try to make you feel like this. So this question requires some serious concern on our part.

If your partner has asked any of these questions about herself—questions about her good qualities and desirable characteristics—we can assume that she is aware of something good about herself and probably has a few qualities that attract people to her.

8. How would you like me to act for the two of us to get along better?

If your partner has asked you this question, she probably feels that you are not as close to her as she would like you to be. She will feel very frustrated if she feels that you are not close enough because she has the deep feeling inside that there could be something great between the two of you. The chances are good that there is something negative between the two of you, but it is better to look at what's positive as well.

9. If people were constantly trying to put me down, what can I do about it?

Many people have the idea that if someone were to try to hurt them or make them feel bad about themselves, they would act right away to defend themselves. But in reality, if someone always makes you feel bad, you will probably just keep trying to avoid that person. For example, if your partner doesn't want you in his life because he doesn't like himself and can't accept his own mistakes, then he will try to get back at you by making you feel guilty for something. Then when you are feeling guilty and insecure about yourself, he will start telling you that it is your fault for not being supportive enough because he needs your understanding.

10. How can I give people more respect than they give themselves?

If you can figure out how to do this, you and your partner will be able to make the most of the relationship. If your partner feels that you respect him more than he respects himself, he will probably feel much better about himself.

These questions are designed to help you respect each other as couples. If you believe that your partner has good qualities, you will want to be close to him. If you are interested in improving your relationship, you can begin by finding out what is holding you back from getting closer to each other.

NOTES

Chapter 5:
Questions on Quality time

Quality time is one of the most important aspects of a relationship. It doesn't have to be fancy or expensive. All you need is each other; and sometimes that's all you need to make things seem right in the world again.

Grab some popcorn, settle down for a cozy night in, and ask each other these questions to get things going! You'll be surprised at what you learn.

1. What do you enjoy doing together?

This question is extremely open-ended, and it will allow both parties to talk about their favorite things to do as a couple. It can be as simple as walking around the block or going out for a milkshake, but it's rare that couples get the chance to discuss little joys like this!

2. Where would you like to go someday?

This question is a good one for those who are married and have already been on various vacations. It's also perfect for those who simply want to travel and need some inspiration! Asking each other where you've always wanted to go is a great way to have fun dreaming and planning your future adventures together.

3. What is your favorite memory of us together?

This question is all about reminiscing. It will allow both partners to share the funniest or most touching moments of your time together. Even if you've heard these moments a million times before, asking this question again is a great way to spark renewed joy and laughter in your relationship!

4. How would most people describe the two of us as a couple?

Couples rarely take the time to stop and think about what others think of them as a unit. This is an opportunity for you both to step back and see how others see you, which can provide insights into the type of people that the two of you are as a couple!

5. Who is the most important person in your life, besides me?

This question is all about getting better acquainted with each other. It will allow you to see how important your partner is to you outside of the relationship. Often, it can spark conflicts because one partner may not appreciate the amount of time the other spends with family or friends. When dealing with this issue in a relationship, it's important for both partners to be open and honest so that these types of conflicts can be addressed early on before they get blown out of proportion.

6. What do you like most about being married?

This question is a fun one that will allow each person to reminisce about the reasons why you got married in the first place. It will provide renewed joy and reason to be grateful that you're together. It's also a good tool for those who may have been together for so long that you've forgotten what you saw in each other in the first place.

7. If I could change one thing about myself, what would it be and why?

This question can ignite a firestorm of honesty which is always needed between partners. If your partner says that he wishes he were taller or she wishes she had bigger boobs, it will make you think about your own self-image and how those things impact the relationship as a whole.

8. Why did we decide to get married in the first place, and how is it working out so far?

This question can be extremely important because it will allow you to see what the big picture in your relationship when you got married. It may reveal that you both expected very different things from marriage, which may lead to an unexpected conflict. It can also provide a good way for both of you to reflect on your individual expectations of marriage before it became a reality.

9. What is the best thing about having kids?

If you have any little ones running around, this question will generate some serious laughs (and probably a few tears). Not only is it a great way to enjoy a night in as parents if you have the kids at home, but it can also be a good way to see just how much the two of you have in common. If your opinions are polar opposites on this topic, some tension needs to be addressed!

10. Where do you see us in five years?

This is another question that allows both partners to step back and look at the big picture. It will allow both parties to reflect on where they see themselves and their relationship going forward. It's also a great tool to provide perspective on how you've both grown in your relationship and whether or not it's heading in a positive direction.

These questions are all great tools to help you get to know each other on an intimate level. They'll spark discussions and allow the two of you to look at your relationship from a different perspective. If you and your partner can answer them together, it will provide a safe place for both of you to share some vulnerability that will strengthen your bond as a couple.

NOTES

Chapter 6:
Questions on How to fight fair

In order to fight fair, you need to have a clear understanding of what is it you are fighting for and why. What is it about the situation that upsets you? Is this an issue that can be resolved through constructive discussion? Do you want to make your partner aware of something they do not realize? Are you trying to change a current behavior pattern by putting pressure on the other person?

Don't focus solely on what's wrong in your relationship. Focus also on the positive aspects and possible solutions; there might just be ways in which both parties could compromise and work together. Whatever your goal is when fighting, be fair and try not to put blame or throw judgmental criticism at each other. This will only cause the other person to react defensively. If your partner is capable of accepting responsibility for his or her actions, you can actually make them feel more secure. If your partner is defensive, try not to take it personally. This is a sign that you have done something wrong and need to correct it.

When fighting fair, remember to listen and understand what the other person has to say before you continue with what you were saying. You may be surprised to find that the root of the argument was not even related to what you originally thought. We often enter into arguments thinking we know exactly why because we tend to focus on ourselves—our own feelings, beliefs and wants—rather than our partner's thoughts and feelings.

Here are questions for couples to ask each other. Use these questions to guide your discussions and try not to get into the same arguments using the same words, each time.

1. What do you consider to be a healthy relationship?

A healthy relationship is one in which the couple has empathy towards each other. They listen to each other and appreciate what they do for each other. They have a sense of mutual trust.

2. What is love? How do you show your partner that you love them? Love is an action, not a feeling. Showing your partner that you love them means taking the time to do little things for them. It could be as simple as doing their laundry or giving them a foot massage.

3. What does intimacy mean to you in a partnership/marriage/relationship and how can we create more intimacy in ours?

4. What is a healthy balance of individuality and togetherness?

5. What would it take for us to move forward and make the changes we want to make in our relationship?

6. Do you think we can make these changes or is it time to move on? (If one or both don't want to work on things, then it's time.)

7. What is respect and how can we show respect in a healthy relationship?

Respect is treating each other with dignity and kindness, no matter what the situation - right or wrong. This includes having patience with one another, listening to each other and considering what the other partner has to say before responding instead of reacting defensively.

8. Why do we have conflict in our relationships?

Conflict occurs whenever there is a difference of opinion or point of view. The main source of conflict is when there is disrespect, or one partner feels as though the other does not appreciate him/her or care about his/her feelings. This can happen when we are under stress, tired or frustrated. One way to prevent this from happening is by being genuine with your words and actions; in other words, mean what you say and do what you say you are going to do!

9. How did our family influence how we handle conflict and deal with each other as adults?

Our families, whether they be immediate or extended, have an immense impact on who we are as individuals. Perhaps one or both of you had a parent who was overly strict and demanding, or perhaps one of your parents was always yelling at you to do well in school (or did not encourage you enough). You felt as though you could never get enough praise. Your family taught you how to deal with conflict in an unhealthy manner; the sooner we learn to deal with conflict positively, the better off we will be in our relationships.

10. How did growing up together or apart affect how we relate to each other as adults? (separated couples only)

It is important to remember that your past does not have to determine your future. When people who are abused and/or neglected come together in a new relationship, they often find themselves repeating the same unhealthy patterns of communication and behavior that they experienced in their families. This is because they had no one in their lives telling them at an early age that what was happening was wrong, and no one teaching them how to deal with conflict in a healthy way.

This is a big reason why people leave their partners; most of the time, it is not because they don't love them or want to be with them but because they can't get out of those unhealthy patterns of behavior and/or they can't stand to see the pain in their partner's eyes.

11. What does intimacy mean to you in a partnership/marriage/relationship and how can we create more intimacy in the relationship?

Intimacy means closeness and connectedness. It is not, as many people think, sexual activity. Too often, couples wait to discuss important issues until after they have had sex. This only allows the issue to fester and grow into something bigger than it was when it started. If you really want a healthy relationship, you have to make time for intimacy.

12. How do we go about setting up boundaries and rules to promote a healthy relationship?

It is important that each person be clear with their partner what their boundaries are and that they respect one another's boundaries as well as those of their extended family and friends! Role-playing is a great tool for helping couples set up boundaries in an easy way that does not hurt anyone's feelings!

13. How do you feel about money? Do you think that it is important to share financial responsibilities?

Money can be an issue in any relationship. Many people never get over their resentment and anger toward their parents for the way they handled money when they were growing up. Some people use money to keep score, while others are afraid that if they have too much, their partner will leave them or take it away, etc. If money is a problem for your partner, then you must deal with it and find a way to make the other person comfortable with the situation!

10. What are your life goals for the next 20 years?

Knowing where you want to be in 5, 10 or 20 years is an important part of any relationship. If both partners share the same goals, then it can help build a rewarding and loving relationship. If one person has no interest in reaching their dreams, then they may resent their partner for holding them back.

You might want to take turns answering the questions. As you talk, listen for underlying feelings and unspoken expectations that need to be understood and resolved. Remember to focus on feelings and not on right/wrong, good/bad or whose fault it is. Keep the discussion focused on issues and not your partner or yourself.

Also note that some of the questions above will be more relevant for couples who have been together for a longer time than those who have been together for just a few months. After all, there is a lot to learn about each other during courtship, but there is even more to learn about each other after many years of marriage. You will want to add more questions based on your situation and experience as well as any concerns you might need to discuss with each other.

It is important that the questions not offend, upset or otherwise trigger your partner in an unhealthy way. If you notice that a question upsets your partner, it is best to replace it with another question.

If you use any these questions in a discussion, record the responses recorded for future reference. It will take time and requires patience but it is possible for both of you to learn and grow from the process of fighting fair. Once fighting fair is understood by both parties, it will only become a matter of time before you realize how much progress you have made together as a couple.

NOTES

Chapter 7:
Questions That Make you Think

Sometimes, our days are so busy that we barely have time to think. And when you're in a relationship, it can be hard to find moments where you can see the big picture and make decisions together. But it's important to set aside some time for this because it will have a huge impact on your relationship. Start by thinking about how you and your partner feel about each other right now in general and then narrow it down to how you feel about specific things like communication, sexuality or relationships with parents and friends. The more you know about each other, the easier it will be to discuss the issues that come up along the way.

When answering these questions about how you feel in general, think about everything, including the little things. Rate your feelings on a scale from 1 to 10. And if you need help deciding how to rank each item, ask yourself these questions: is this feeling something I am totally comfortable with? How much do I support it? Does this feeling make me want to change anything in my life?

To get started with these questions, ask yourself:

1. Am I making a decision about my health because I understand my options?

This question will help you focus on whether or not you really understand the options that have been presented to you. If your decision isn't based on understanding and knowledge, it will be hard for your partner to trust that you're making the right decision for yourself and the relationship.

If you need more information, ask your doctor or a trusted family member or friend to help explain things in a way that makes sense to you.

2. Am I making the decision that is best for me?

This question will help you focus on what's most important. It will help you think about your wants and needs, and the wants and needs of your partner. It will also make sure you're not being influenced by things that have nothing to do with your health or treatment plan.

If your decision isn't what's best for both of you, talk with your doctor or a trusted friend so they can help to make sure it fits with all the other parts of your life.

3. Have I thought about how my decision will affect my partner?

You may feel that you're making a decision for yourself and not your partner, but your partner's opinion matters. They have the right to decide how they feel about your decisions and whether or not they are okay with it. If you aren't thinking about how your decision will affect them, it might not be the best decision for either of you.

If you don't know how your partner feels about what you're doing or would like to include them more in this process, talk with them.

4. Have I explained the treatment decision to my partner?

You may not want to tell your partner every detail about the problem, but it is important to talk it over with them. Your partner may be able to help you understand things like cost, the process of treatment, and the potential side effects. Plus, you might find out that your partner is uncomfortable with a certain choice or may have questions of their own.

If they don't understand what you're doing or don't approve, don't be afraid to talk about their feelings and try to come up with something that works for both of you.

5. Will my decision be good for me in the long term?

This question will help you focus on what will happen after your treatment. It will make sure that you're not just thinking about what happens immediately, but also down the road.

Keep in mind that health problems change over time, so you may need to get more treatment or have a different option later on.

If you feel like your choice doesn't address future issues, talk with your doctor, a friend or partner about it.

6. Have I thought about how this decision fits into my life as a whole?

Think about things like school, work plans and social activities that are important to you. Are there other things in your life that may make this decision harder to accomplish?

For example, some of the decisions you might need to make are hard if you have a job, kids, or a family. But if your decision fits into all the parts of your life, it will be easier to follow through.

If this decision doesn't fit in with the rest of what's going on in your life, however, talk with your doctor or trusted friend about it so they can help you find a different option.

7. Do I understand how to take care of myself if I decide to have treatment?

Some treatments can be hard and may need special follow-up care. It's important that you know what your treatment will be like, who will help you with it, and what kind of follow-up care you'll need.

Sometimes this information is hard to find, so talk about what kinds of things you'll need to do after the treatment is over.

8. Am I sure about my choice?

Ask yourself if there are any doubts in your mind about making a decision now. If you're not sure whether to have treatment or not, you should talk with your doctor or someone you trust. After a while, decide if you'll have treatment or not. If you decide to wait for now, add the following question to your list:

9. Have I talked about my decision with family and friends?

If there are things in your life that are important to other people (like your friends, family, and religion), involving them can make things easier. It can also help with making big decisions (like whether to have treatment or not).

How do you get started? You may feel a lot of pressure to "just get started." But take it easy because you're the one who is going to be doing all the work, and none of it has to be done all at once.

Next, follow these seven steps:

1. Make a list. Write down the things that are important or interesting for you at this point. Your list could include things like your disease and its symptoms, treatment decisions, or important life questions (like what kind of work you want to do or where in the world you want to live).

2. Make a timeline. When are you going to think about your choices? Maybe you want to make a list of questions at the beginning of each week, or maybe you want to talk things over with your partner once a month. Then decide when you're going to review and update your list so that it's always ready when you need it.

3. Pick up the pace. As time passes, some of these questions may feel less important or urgent, so don't stress if it takes longer than expected to finish your whole list; just do what works best for now and adjust as needed later on.

4. Keep it all in one place. If you're going to have more than one list, keep them together so all your questions are easy to find. Maybe you want to keep a notebook with your list of questions or put your questions on sticky notes that are easy to move around.

5. Share the load. It can be good to talk about big issues with friends and family who care about what happens next or who can offer a different perspective on your future plans. But remember that it's your decision so don't let anyone else make it for you, especially if they don't know what's best for you or your relationship.

6. Give yourself some space. It can be hard to think about a lot of things all at once, and you might find it easier to think about some parts of your list one at a time. If that works for you, schedule time: I'll work on my list on Mondays and Wednesdays from 12:00-1:00 (or whatever works best for you).

7. Take charge of your own health care by getting the information you need and make sure that all your questions are answered before making a decision.

After answering these questions about your health, feelings and views about relationships and life in general, take some time to discuss what it was like to answer them. Get an idea of your partner's responses and how those views are different or similar to yours. Then put these questions away for a little while and work on other exercises.

While you're both working on other exercises, stop thinking about the list of questions and try to let go of whatever feelings or thoughts they brought up. When you're ready to move back to this list, go through them one at a time so that your partner has a chance to answer them too.

If you find yourself getting upset as you think about answering these questions, try breathing slowly (inhaling and exhaling for five counts each) until you feel more relaxed. If that doesn't help, try to distract yourself by thinking pleasant thoughts or do something that takes your mind off the stressful situation. For example, you might try talking to a trusted friend or doing things you enjoy that don't involve thinking about your health.

Making the decision: finally, when you reach the point where you feel ready to make a decision (and have made sure that all your questions have been answered), consult with someone who has gone through this process and whose opinion you value. Choose someone unbiased and supportive of your decision, if possible. This person can be your counselor, doctor, a friend or family member. They will help you think about your situation and get a fresh perspective on the issue.

When you're ready to make a decision about your health, it's important to make it on the basis of good information and not just strong feelings. Use the following questions to guide you through the decision-making process. These questions are designed for after you have made some choices about treatment options and want to make sure your decisions are based on solid information and good thinking.

When dealing with important issues like these, it may be hard for you to keep your focus on the right things. If that's the case, take a break and come back to the questions when you feel ready. Or talk with someone you trust who can help to keep your thoughts grounded or find another way to get through it.

NOTES

Chapter 8:
Questions on Conflicts with In-laws and Extended Family Members

Relationships with in-laws and extended family members can be a source of stress and frustration for everyone involved. In this chapter, we'll look at the root causes of these conflicts, potential solutions to reduce future conflict, and learn how to have better communication with each other.

Are you interested in knowing how to deal with your spouse's in-laws or extended family members? Take a look at our list of 10 questions for couples!

1. Does you feel as strongly about the issue as I do?

This question could be the most important one on the list. It is vital to figure out if your partner is as invested in solving the issue as you are. Perhaps you have differing opinions on dealing with certain conflicts. Discuss these differences and how you can come to a solution that works for both of you instead of going your separate ways.

2. How would you describe your relationship with my family members?

Sometimes your partner may be unwilling to open up about his or her family relationships due to various reasons, including fear of creating conflict or embarrassment, or anything else that may cause distress. Be patient and find a quiet time to have a non-confrontational conversation with your partner where you can discuss your concerns.

3. How does you feel when around my family members?

Sometimes conflicts between family members may be related to differences in cultural upbringing or opinions. For example, one spouse may have limited contact with his or her parents due to differences in religion or lifestyle, while the other one maintains frequent contact and visits often. If you ask this question and find that your partner is uncomfortable when you are around their extended family, it could be because he or she feels embarrassed about the differences in opinion, lifestyle or culture between the two families.

3. What would you like to see happen in our relationship with family members?

The answer will let you know what your partner thinks about the current state of his or her relationship with his or her relatives. You can then work together to find a solution that is mutually beneficial for everyone involved.

4. What have you done so far about this issue?

If your partner feels as strongly about the issue as you do, it may be because he or she has already brought it up in conversation with family members before and even come up with a solution to fix it. If this has happened before, make sure to understand what steps have been taken so far and if they were successful.

5. What will you do if I don't want to deal with the issue anymore?

It is important to know what both of you will do if one of you is unwilling to continue dealing with this issue. If multiple attempts have been made at solving the problem and it still exists, this may be a good time to re-evaluate your relationship.

6. What else would you like to share on this topic?

This question is useful for couples seriously considering taking action in resolving a family conflict or who are already taking action. You can discuss your plans and make sure that both parties are on board before making any decisions.

7. Are there any ways you would like to improve our communication?

There are times when conflict arises due to poor communication between the couple, and extended family members become collateral damage. Sometimes, the best way to avoid getting into conflicts with family members is to talk about it with your partner first. If talking about family conflict does not work out, you may need professional help. Seeking a couple's counselor could be a good step forward in resolving disputes with your partner's relatives. The counselor can help you identify potential causes of conflict and how to deal with them once they arise.

8. How do you feel when we spend time together without your family members?

Some conflicts between families may be due to one partner feeling neglected by the other, or vice versa. Try doing fun activities with each other — without the interference of family — and see if your relationship improves. This will let you know if your partner is comfortable enough to spend quality time with just you. If the answer is no, perhaps you should try spending less time with his or her family and more time with each other.

9. What do you want to be said about our relationship with your family members?

Everyone wants to feel validated. Once you know that the topic of conversation is not going to end in an argument, it will be easier for both of you to talk and come up with a solution that will improve your relationship with extended family members.

10. What is the most important thing for both of us to remember when dealing with this issue?

This question is helpful if the conflict seems overwhelming and you both need something to take away from it. This way, if one or both of you forget about what was discussed after a while, talking about it again will be easier. After this conversation, hopefully you will have a better idea of how to mend your relationship with your partner's family members. If talking about it doesn't work out, you can see a couple's counselor to help improve communication and avoid future conflicts.

NOTES

Chapter 9:
Questions on Money Matters

Getting along with someone's financial habits can be just as important as getting along with them. Just like a couple has different tastes in food and music, they also might have different ideas about how they spend their money. Even in a relationship where both people earn an income, there is always the possibility that one person spends more than the other. This can be a sensitive area for some couples, and it can also cause resentment – and possibly even arguments! That's why it's important to talk about money issues together.

The next time you're together, find a place where you can have a conversation in private. Make sure that you have enough privacy to talk comfortably. If your partner is not very open about money issues, you might want to start off the conversation by asking what he or she thinks about money matters. Even if your partner is more open about their feelings on the subject, it can feel more natural if one person asks questions first.

If you want to have a friendly conversation about money, it can be helpful to have a few discussion points lined up. Here are some of the most important money topics that people might like to discuss:

1. What are your priorities when it comes to money?

This question will help you to understand what is important to your partner when it comes to spending and saving. A person's first answer might not be their final answer, so it is important to follow up with the following question:

2. How do you want to handle money as a couple?

If there are current habits you don't agree with, then it will be helpful to talk about how you can handle these differences moving forward. If the person you are dating has different spending habits than you, it is also helpful to talk about how much of an influence these differences might have on the future of the relationship.

3. Does my spending bother you?

This is a good question to ask if one of you is more frugal or spendthrift than the other. This could cause problems in the future, especially if one person likes to splurge and the other likes to save.

4. How can we work together on our money issues?

This helps both people understand how they can compromise moving forward. It also helps couple focus on only their money issues and not on other important relationship issues as well.

5. What are your financial goals?

It is a good idea for both partners in a relationship to have an understanding of each other's' financial goals, even if they are very different. If a couple has different goals, they should figure out how these goals will affect the relationship moving forward.

If you are dating someone you know casually, there are even more important issues to talk about. These include where each person sees their financial future in a year or two, and how much responsibility they want in the relationship. If both people earn money, it is also helpful to talk about who will be responsible for the household expenses.

These points might help your conversation along, or you can come up with other conversation points that are more relevant. The important thing is to have an open conversation and be honest with each other about your feelings on money matters.

The financial health of a household can be tied to the overall health of the relationship. Couples have a higher risk of divorce if they are neither financially satisfied nor financially compatible. One way to assess the health of a relationship is by looking at your credit reports, which provide a wealth of information about your relationship status and spending habits.

The lesson here: don't give yourself more credit than you deserve, and don't blow up your past or present successes out of proportion. Remember that you are just as fallible as your cohorts and future endeavors are no guarantee of success. Be patient with yourself and your money; try to be realistic in your expectations. It's easy to let the past determine the present and future.

That's why it's important not to compare yourself with others, especially when it comes to finances. The truth is that there really is no right or wrong way to handle money, and it's all about what works best for you. While there are always new methods of saving money coming out, the most important thing is to find what works best for you and your family. Here are more questions.

1. How would you describe our money situation? How do you feel about it?

2. Have there been any major changes in our finances recently? What caused them? Where do you hope they'll lead?

3. Are there things in your relationship that cause disagreements about money or make it difficult to talk about it?

4. What kind of help or advice do you want from regarding our money situation?

5. How can I support you financially?

6. Is there anything else we should discuss about our money situation?

If you have trouble talking to your partner about money, now is the time for a discussion! You might not always see eye-to-eye with your partner when it comes to financial decisions, but that doesn't mean that you shouldn't talk about the subject. After all, it is a very important thing in a relationship and needs to stay healthy for the relationship to stay healthy. If you're afraid to start a discussion about money because you don't know how to talk about it, try doing it in a fun way!

NOTES

Chapter 10:
Questions on Intimacy

Yes, intimacy is important! It's the foundation of our relationships and allows us to experience satisfying connections with the people we love. Intimacy is also a dynamic process that involves all of our senses: physical, emotional, intellectual, and spiritual. It means paying attention to what someone is saying while they are speaking, but also noticing their tone of voice, body language, and facial expressions.

Intimate communication goes beyond talking; in fact, it often happens through touch (like a hug or a kiss) or when we connect with someone "viscerally" by listening closely to their words and letting ourselves feel their emotions.

Intimacy isn't easy especially in the early stages of relationships. You may be wondering if you can really trust this person who seems so different from you. You'll need to be patient and open and take the time to get to know each other. If your partner wants the same thing, then intimacy can grow in the relationship, and may even get better over time.

If you want more intimacy in your relationship, you both need to be willing to share what turns you on as well as what turns you off; that is the only way you can truly find out what feels good for each partner. For instance, if he tells you that he enjoys watching pornography, or she reveals she has a foot fetish, those things may turn off or weird out a lot of people.

If you want to become more intimate, you need to be willing to reveal things you have a hard time talking about with just anyone (or maybe even at all). The more open and honest communication you can share, the closer you will feel.

However, giving and receiving intimacy is often a two-way street. If you want your partner to give of him or herself sexually, then in turn you need to be willing to open yourself up sexually as well. If your partner has sexual fantasies they would like fulfilled but won't ask for them, you need to be willing to fulfill their needs. It's important to have fun with each other, so have fun answering these questions! Ask them of each other.

1. When you think of me as your partner, what are the first things that come to mind? What associations do you have with me? What do I represent in your life? What do I mean to you and how so?

2. Were there moments when we were close to each other that you recall as being particularly special, romantic or intimate? Can you share those moments with me now? How did they make you feel?

3. In what ways have you been intimate that are important to you? Have there been times when you felt especially close to me?

4. What do you feel is the most important element of an intimate relationship? Is it sexual, emotional closeness, or something else? Why do you feel that way?

5. What are the differences in being intimate with a partner compared to a regular friendship? Are there differences in being intimate in a long-term relationship versus a new relationship or hooking up with someone for one night?

6. How often do you find yourselves not sharing enough "inner" things about yourself? What keeps you from being more open and vulnerable with me? At what points during our relationship have you felt especially open and intimate?

7. How much of your self-worth and sense of being has the relationship with me come to represent? What have been the most intense moments in our relationship?

8. What is it like for you to share something with me that you haven't told another person before? Be concrete. How does it feel? Are there things that you have tried not telling me, but I make you feel comfortable talking about?

9. How do different types of communication relate to intimacy: physical touch, sexual activities, intellectual connection, emotional sharing, spiritual connection?

10. What are the things that you do that allow for a deepening of intimacy? What do you need to do differently in order for the level of intimacy to grow for us?

11. How does the degree of intimacy in our relationship differ as a man and a woman? When does it work better? When is it worse?

12. What are good ways to introduce more emotional and physical closeness in our relationship? Be specific.

13. What are some of the challenges you have faced when trying to be more intimate in our interactions, in general and sexually?

14. How do you express your feelings about the closeness that we share?

15. What are some of the most intense moments in our relationship? Be concrete. How does it feel?

16. What has been most challenging about sharing sexual intimacy together? How can you overcome it?

17. Is there anything I have asked that made you feel nervous, uncomfortable, or a little self-conscious? Would you like to share with me what it was and why it made you feel that way?

18. Is there anything I have asked that you really liked talking about or being intimate with me? Would you like to share what that was and why it made you feel good?

19. Do you genuinely enjoy spending time together? What are some of your favorite activities together? What do you feel is important about doing these activities regularly with each another?

20. When you recall your best experiences in a relationship, what comes to mind? What are some of the most intense moments when you thinking back over the years at the beginning, middle and end of the relationship or a particular phase in it?

NOTES

Chapter 11:
Questions on Reconnecting with Your Spouse

This chapter includes questions to get to know your partner better. They are designed to be used during personal time together. If you choose to answer them all, consider spending 30 minutes talking about the questions one night a week for 6 weeks. Or if you choose to only answer a few, consider picking questions you would like to work on for the coming week and talking about them at a time that works best for both. Make sure you are in a quiet place where the two of you can sit comfortably. Read the questions (there is one for each of you) and ask each other the questions in order. Discuss what was said and how you feel about it. You don't have to answer all the questions at once. You can pick the ones you want to work on together.

Here we go!

In your relationship, it's important to be open with each other and share things about yourself that you wouldn't share with others. Take turns answering and try not to hold back! If it makes you uncomfortable, that's a good thing because sharing feelings may help you both better understand each other.

1. What is one physical thing that you love about yourself?

This question is designed to help you understand what your partner likes about his/her body. Some of you are probably thinking, "I'm happy with my body," or something similar. If so, ask the follow-up question: what one physical thing would you like to change about yourself? (You could say, "What's one thing you'd like to change about your appearance?") This will get both of you thinking and talking about physical attributes.

2. How is our sex life?

This question is designed to further tap into feelings that may be difficult for both of you to talk about. Try to relax and share what you feel. If you are uncomfortable with the question, think about what things in the bedroom could be improved. If you choose to answer this question together, it may be helpful to answer what do we do that you like but I don't? Could we try that?

3. What do I do that frustrates / annoys / bothers you?

The purpose of this question is to identify frustrations in the relationship so they can be addressed and worked on. This will also give you insight into your spouse's personality and help the two of you become closer by becoming more understanding of each other. For example, if you find out that being late frustrates your spouse, arrange to leave early or have more communication about the plan ahead of time.

4. Do I do things that have made you proud?

Many of you are probably thinking, "Yes! Of course!" But there's a great truth in this question: if your spouse made you proud for doing something in the past, then he/she will continue to do so in the future! It is important to understand what your spouse thinks is a win-win situation and what makes him/her feel good about himself/herself as well as the relationship.

5. What do I need to be more comfortable around you?

This question is designed to get you talking about things that might be uncomfortable. For many of you, it will touch on sexual feelings. Don't be afraid to share "intimate" feelings with each other. Remember that the point of this book is to have a loving and intimate relationship in which you are comfortable sharing your inner thoughts and desires.

6. What are some things I can do for you that will have an impact on your life?

This question is designed to help us all think about how we can make a positive difference. We want our spouses to feel like they can count on us and that we truly care about them. It is important we do things to show our support. What are some things that your spouse does that have made a positive impact on your life? What would you like them to do in the future?

7. What would you never want me to do?

This question is designed to help you think about boundaries in the relationship and respecting those boundaries. There may be something you want to do, but because of your spouse's personality or past experiences, it might not be something he/she feels good about. This is an important area for discussion. It's better that those feelings come up now than later when both of you have invested more in the relationship.

8. What would you do if I got fired from my job?

This question is designed to provoke feelings and thoughts about what life would be like if one of you were not in the same place. This can be a difficult question for some because it deals with an unpleasant subject that might cause feelings of sadness, fear, or guilt. It is good to talk about these things now so that you understand each other's reactions and plans ahead of time.

9. What's your happiest memory with me?

This question is designed to help you focus on positive memories from the past, present, and future. It is important to identify the things that made your relationship stronger in the past, as well as the things that will make your relationship stronger in the future. Even though this is a tough question, try not to be negative when talking about the memories you have. It is important to remember that even though people change over time, your love for each other should not change.

This brings us back to the importance of communicating in a positive way and remembering our love for one another.

10. How did I make you feel during _____ (a past experience)?

This question is designed to get you thinking about how you can communicate with each other better in the future by learning from past experiences. It is important to remember that you have different communication styles. It may be that in the past, your spouse reacted in a negative way to something you did because his/her communication style was different than yours. You want to learn about each other's communication styles so you can talk about things in an effective manner going forward.

After going through these 10 questions, it is good to go back and focus on the first one. You should be able to remember what your spouse said to you in response to each of the 10 questions. This will make it easier for you both to communicate with each other going forward. It is important for you to remember that by doing this exercise, there was a deeper level of communication and understanding between you. You were able to talk about things that can be uncomfortable for some couples and were still able to have a good, positive conversation about them. This kind of communication will help your relationship grow stronger from this point forward.

NOTES

Chapter 12:
Day-to-day Conflict Resolution

How you handle conflict is a direct reflection of what kind of partner you are to each other. Do you let your partner know that when they say _____, it makes me feel _____? Do you ever bring up topics that need to be addressed outside an argument? These are just some examples of questions that should be asked if you want to foster a healthy connection with your spouse.

This book explores 10 important questions for couples and offers insights on how to answer them. Trust is the foundation of a healthy relationship. Do you know if your partner has an online presence? Is he or she active on social media? As with everything, check the comments for any signs of negativity.

When couples have the same vision of what they want to achieve together, their dreams are more likely to be realized. For example, if one partner wants to start a business or buys a house and the other is unwilling (or has different plans), then that partnership may dissolve. Firmly aligning your goals in life will help you make decisions together as a couple.

These are just some examples of the questions that should be asked if you want to foster a healthy connection with your spouse. You already know how important communication is in any relationship. It is the foundations of all good relationships, and it applies whether you're married or not.

Remember that when answering these questions, honesty is always the best policy, and when in doubt, err on the side of carefully considering your words.

It's normal for partners to disagree sometimes (even married couples). With this question, ask yourself whether you find yourself falling into that trap often. If so, it may be valuable to have a conversation about how to approach conflict more effectively in the future.

If your partner constantly brings up past mistakes (or yours), it may be time to talk about how to approach the subject differently. A relationship is a living thing, and it's important to nurture it properly.

How do you feel when you get in fights? Are they draining? Does it seem like you're repeating yourself? Do you have confidence that your partner is listening to what you say (even if he or she doesn't agree)? These questions should be discussed. Ask yourself if your goals in life are compatible with your partner's.

This applies to both short-term and long-term goals. For example, if one partner decides to take a year off from school, the other might not be on board with that decision. As a result, problems arise when one is trying to move forward and the other is trying to hold him or her back.

If you have different visions of what you want in 10 years, then talk it out. Maybe your partner wants children, and you want a career. Maybe your partner wants to live on the beach, and you want to live in the mountains. As long as both partners understand each other's life dreams, then they're more likely to come together and decide on a compromise that works for both of them.

NOTES

Conclusion

There are many ways to communicate in a loving relationship. As an example, consider the "no contact" rule. It basically dictates that partners must separate themselves from each other during arguments or other intense discussions and not initiate or accept contact until they have cooled off. If this rule is not followed, much harm can be caused to the relationship, especially if the argument escalates to physical violence.

It is also important that people understand why they argue with their partners in the first place. It helps them realize what could be causing conflict within their relationship and what they can do to work together to fix it before it gets worse. There is a vast array of methods to resolve conflicts, from mediation to couples counseling. Whatever route people decide to take, it is extremely important that they are aware of the potential consequences. If not, a small disagreement could escalate into something more serious.

It is also important for partners to remember that there are some things that can never be solved. If this happens, it is best to learn how to carry on with life without dwelling on the argument as if there is no hope of a resolution. This will allow them to avoid getting caught up in the conflict and possibly causing further harm to the relationship as a result of their refusal to compromise.

The whole point of communication is for couples to understand each other and work out differences together rather than losing patience or taking sides against one another.

The list of 20 questions provided aims to help couples understand and appreciate each other, talk about their feelings, listen to each other more and share their thoughts.

These questions are for all types of relationships - same gender or others, married or not married. We also encourage you to use the answers as a starting point for discussions about things not included in this list.

Thank you.

Healing from Infidelity

*How to Cope with an Affair
and Fix a Broken Heart*

Introduction

How does one define infidelity in a relationship? Here, the spouses might have a challenge. Typically, when we talk about infidelity, we refer to sexual affairs. It is true to say that sexual affairs are the most destructive form of cheating, but there are other ways that people become unfaithful in relationships and marriages. Emotional cheating involves getting too close to someone other than your spouse or partner to the extent that you lose interest in the primary relationship. Emotional infidelity can be online or face-to-face - but without sexual contact.

Some acts we consider small might lead to huge infidelity actions. It is therefore important to safeguard our relationships. Most couples avoid discussing infidelity in details for various reasons. First, in the initial stages of a relationship, the partners might feel too in love, hence they overlook the impact of infidelity in their commitment. A couple might avoid bringing the topic up in fear that one person will misinterpret the other as untrusting.

A couple might express to each other that cheating is unacceptable but then fail to describe what cheating means in their terms. For example, one person might consider chatting with strangers a good thing while the other finds it offensive; since there is no absolute definition, the couples will inevitably disagree.

It is important for couples to sit down and agree on what is inappropriate and behavior. Such a discussion cannot be easy, but at least you will have a common ground to work from. Be ready to have different views on the topic, but the best thing is to come to a common ground together. There are things one partner might mention, and the other feels they are overreactions, but the two people need to understand each other's needs. Everyone needs to realize that no matter what their feelings are towards a particular topic, the other person might not see it the same way; therefore, this person could dismiss the suggestion and fail to change accordingly. In such a case, you will be required to decide whether you can live with the person or not.

Typically, infidelity is defined as the violation of a sexual agreement between two people in a relationship. Under the philosophy of romanticism, sex is not just a physical act; it includes the central symbol and summation of love. Since the mid-eighteenth century, romanticism has been centered on the human understanding of love. Before this philosophy came into being, people fell in love and had sex, but they did not see these two acts as having a shared link. People could have sex and not be in love while others could love and not get intimate. The philosophy of romanticism sets sex as the crowning moment of love whereby one expresses his/her devotion for the other through physical, sexual encounters.

Rather than conspire to meet with an affair partner in person, these days interested parties can connect via text, email, or online forums. They can seek out pleasures from strangers or feast on a buffet of on-demand pornography and go about their daily lives. The recent surge of cyber affairs remains a grey area in the subject of infidelity.

Do cyber affairs really count as affairs? If we define infidelity as hidden emotional and/or sexual interactions with people other than your partner, then yes, online affairs do count. However, if we define cheating as physical, sexual contact, then no, these online encounters might not meet the usual criteria.

Whether these types of affairs differ from those in days of old, the damage they inflict is much the same. We have begun to categorize that damage—in the offended partner's experience—as not just painful but also traumatic. Although not officially classified as a disorder, post-infidelity stress disorder is something many offended partners experience. The symptoms are similar to those of post-traumatic stress disorder (PTSD): people report trouble sleeping, intrusive thoughts, constant triggers, and a range of emotions from extreme rage to numbness.

The outlook continues to be rather bleak: the risk of an unfaithful partner cheating again is high, and the recovery rate for couples is low. That said, those couples who work to recover and build a new relationship, instead of trying to "get things back to normal," tend to have a better chance at a fresh start.

How do we define infidelity? Does it count if a married woman brings doughnuts to her single office assistant every morning? What if a partner texts their best friend from college throughout the day but has little or no communication with their spouse? If there is no touching involved, does emotional intimacy count? What qualifies as "emotional intimacy," anyway?

Chapter 1:
Understanding Infidelity

Infidelity is one of the greatest tragedies that befall relationships. When we are young, relationships are easy and love is simple. Love at a young age consists of loving parents, best friends, and peers. There are hardly any complications and serious obligations arising from the word "love" when one is young. However, as we get older and settle in serious relationships, consisting of spouses and long-term commitments, the words love and intimacy get more complicated; they come with expectations and commitments. We are expected to meet the needs of our partners while they ensure that our needs are also met.

What are The Causes of Infidelity?

Certain things lead to infidelity. They can be classified as (but not limited to) physical, emotional, and practical causes.

Physical Causes

Some of the partners engaging in acts of infidelity cite sexual dissatisfaction with their partners. They state their reason for straying is that sex is not as they expected, so they tend to feel unfulfilled. The straying partners may state that they do not receive enough pleasure or even reach a climax as they would like. In other cases, they might state a lack of passion and chemistry as their reason for infidelity. In the latter case, the straying spouse might be comparing their current sex to what they had when the relationship was just starting. Normally, sex in the initial stages of a relationship is wild, exciting, and liberated; therefore, couples can misconstrue the honeymoon phase of sex as passion and chemistry.

Consequently, a person may be tempted to look for that passion in a new partner instead of identifying ways to relight the chemistry in his/her relationship. Seeking sexual satisfaction outside a relationship just because it is boring or different from expectation is like engaging in drugs, gambling, shopping, and other quick-fix options to escape reality. You will still have to look at real life and evaluate the causes and consequences. The belief that having sex with someone who does not know you allows a certain level of freedom lacking in a formal relationship fuels infidelity. The need for hot and free sex with an anonymous person is another reason why people give for engaging in infidelity.

Emotional Causes

One of the most mentioned and blamed causes of infidelity is emotional disconnection. A person engaging in infidelity will cute feeling unappreciated and sad in the relationship, therefore looking for consolation outside it. Emotional disconnection can lead to secondary feelings such as resentment and anger, further leading to both emotional and physical affairs. An emotional affair may appear like a friendship at first but gradually develops into a serious level of intimacy where personal information gets shared about unhappiness and dissatisfaction in the primary relationship. The "friend" takes on a serious role in the plans of the new partner and becomes a substitute for former thoughts and fantasies.

Practical Causes

Over the years, people have started questioning the practicality of romanticism. A good number of people from the younger generation have questioned the benefits of monogamy. Consequently, they choose relationships and lifestyles that are less monogamous. However, such choices have brought on challenges given the lack of a clear roadmap on open relationships. People in open relationships have their own set of rules, and if one person deviates from them, it brings on feelings of betrayal and hurt. The unfortunate part for couples believing in polygamy is that they make a lot of mistakes when applying the rules.

Does infidelity mean the end of a relationship or love? Infidelity will yield different results for different people. Some relationships will come to an end, while others will thrive. Many couples can tolerate the hurt but might never thrive. The results depend on the individuals and the cause. In some relationships, the spouses will find a reason to turn everything around and start the commitment afresh, while others will find this as cause for separation. Either way, most of the relationships that end because of infidelity have other unresolvable underlying factors. Ending the relationship will cause a lot of heartaches, but if it is the best option for the two people, then they have to accept it. However, choosing to heal the relationship and move on will take time, brutal honesty, reflection, and mighty dedication from both parties.

Is infidelity the only hurtful thing in a relationship? No, infidelity is not the only thing that breaks up relationships. Typically, affairs will cause devastating emotions, but they are not the main way of destroying what you have. When one assesses the causes of infidelity, he/she will realize that an affair is just a symptom of a breakage as well as a cause.

There are thousands of other ways that people break their relationships, for instance, by withholding affection and love, failing to approve of one another, being judgmental in a negative way, or criticizing each other frequently. Almost everyone in a relationship, regardless of how committed and loving they are, will engage in one act of relationship breaking. We should pay attention to our spouses so we notice when their needs and patterns change.

How does infidelity happen?

First, infidelity/cheating is a devastating act of betrayal. However, it can also be a sign of loss, loneliness, and the need for autonomy, novelty, intimacy, power, affection. It boils down to the need to be loved, desired, and wanted. All these needs are valid and important. They do not represent a lack of self-reliance or neediness in any way. They are the reason we come together, fall in love, and choose to stay with our partners, but they are also the main reasons we fall out of love.

The best part of being human is when we are connected with other people, especially the ones we love, adore, and feel connected to wholeheartedly. The human need for connection, love, intimacy, and validation are primal. They are hard-wired into us and cannot be ignored, denied, or pushed down. They can never disappear. Consequently, if these needs are left unmet for too long, the relationship will experience a tear wide enough for someone else to walk in and claim to be able to meet those needs. If a stranger starts meeting any of these important needs, intimacy, alchemy, desire, and the attraction will grow in the intruder.

When a person has an important need that goes unmet for too long, there are only two options—and I mean only two. The person either lets go of the need completely or changes the environment to meet it, which applies to every human being. If the need is subtle, we can ignore it; if it is basic, then we have to meet it one way or another. This will create a fault in the relationship. Hence the temptation to change the existing conditions and find another person to address the unmet needs.

Affairs are not usually about wanting the intruder; rather, it is about the way they can meet the needs. If the person having an affair had a choice, it would be to have his/her partner meet the need instead of the intruder. The cheater does not want to hurt the spouse–that is why they do it in secret. However, life is complicated, and things do not always work out the way we want. Needs are demanding, and the desire to cheat gets heightened. When an affair happens, chances are one of the following three things have happened:

- Something is missing in the relationship, but the partners are not aware of what it is.

- Something is missing, and the person knows what it is; for instance, a need has been hungry for too long, but the two people lack openness and honesty in the relationship.

- There are repeated attempts to address the unmet needs, but they are all unsuccessful; thus, the spouse has to look for comfort from outside.

Sometimes, these needs are not the result of weaknesses in the relationship, but rather dissatisfaction within the self. Some people cheat even when they are in a happy relationship.

When to Seek Help?

Most people agree that a sexual affair is definitely an act of infidelity, but what about sending frisky messages? What if your partner makes several loans and incurs a large debt without you knowing it? Does engaging in cybersex with someone other than your husband or wife constitute an affair? Does connecting with a former partner on social media or having an online dating profile even though you are already in a relationship count as infidelity?

Research authorized by Deseret News found different answers when a thousand people were asked about what defines "cheating." The majority of surveyed (71%-76%) said that having sexual contact with someone aside from your partner would always be counted as cheating. However, a slimmer majority thought that having an online dating profile (63%) or sending frisky texts or chats to someone other than your partner (51%) should always be considered as cheating. The issue is more elliptical when following or befriending an ex on social media: 16% said it was cheating as always, 45% thought it was sometimes cheating, and 39% answered that it's never cheating.

Chapter 2:
Protecting your Marriage and Family from Infidelity

Some marriages survive infidelity. But can your marriage survive it? That vital question is one that only you can answer because your recovery from your infidelity lies squarely in the hands of you and your partner.

But either way, it's going to take some blood, sweat and tears. Your trust has been severely violated, and nobody bounces back from that as if nothing had happened. You loved, and for that love you received deception, betrayal, and lies. You were treated like a troublesome inconvenience rather than the loving partner you believed yourself to be.

How will it be possible for you ever to trust again, to feel comfortable in any relationship, much less one with your betrayer of a spouse. Will you ever be comfortable feeling what love is supposed to engender?

How will you ever get back what you lost? How will you ever know if you had, in the first place, the love that you thought you did?

Was it all an illusion? Was it all a mistake? Did he/she ever really care for you? Was there ever a time when you weren't being made a dupe by your own inability (or unwillingness?) to see the lie behind the "love"?

Are you gonna be able to trust love again?

Statistics show that almost two-thirds of marriages in which one (or both) partners have an affair don't survive the affair; the majority of such couples officially divorce one to two years afterward. This means that there is a fairly long period of time during which the couple looks for possible ways out of the troubles in which they find themselves—where, in other words, they give their relationship a chance to heal. But nearly two-thirds of the time, that chance fails.

Reasons for not Getting Over an Affair

There are six primary reasons:

1. They don't get the proper help. They try to fix themselves when what they need is a trained counselor with experience helping couples get through that critical first year or two following a discovered affair. There are things that couples can do on their own. Surviving infidelity is rarely one of them.

2. They stay in survival mode. Instead of moving forward, the couple stays in what amounts to a state of shock, hoping or assuming that their relationship will somehow magically heal itself. They talk about the infidelity from time to time—a conversation usually started with the betrayed partner—but they rarely come up with any ideas, plans, or agreement about how to go productively forward.

3. They stay the course. Often couples stay together in spite of infidelity not because they love one another but because they'd basically rather pretend that the affair never happened than disturb the status quo. They stay together for the children, for their property, for their careers—for a whole host of reasons having nothing to do with the emotional core of the relationship. But such unhappy, post-affair unions

rarely hold together. People want and need a genuine loving relationship too much to typically be able to sustain the illusion that they can carry on without it.

4. They can't stop fighting. The affair launches a war which, lacking anything resembling constructive and ongoing peace talks, relentlessly continues skirmish after skirmish, battle after battle, until finally there is nothing left of what once was.

5. Suspicion reigns supreme. The aggrieved spouse is constantly tracking, inspecting, suspecting, testing, and trying to trap the husband who did her wrong. As far as she is concerned, he can now do no right. And since healing is right, hers isn't exactly a helpful position to maintain.

6. The revenge binges. The betrayed partner gets revenge by also cheating, believing this will restore balance, and ultimately peace, to her damaged relationship. It never does.

Note: It is quite amazing how often betrayed, hurt women, when in a state of panic about losing their partner and marriage, think that getting pregnant will bind their estranged partner to them when, in fact, pregnancy and a new baby are very stressful for both partners, and stress is a well-known risk factor for infidelity. A baby should arrive at a time when the relationship is defined by happiness and mutual attachment, not by stress and uncertainty. In my twenty years of practice as a psychologist, I have never seen getting pregnant work as a means of saving a failing marriage. So, if you are thinking about taking this course, DO NOT. Countless women before you have tried it, and it has never helped.

It is critical that as a couple, you understand that what the two of you do together in response to the infidelity is significantly more important than the actual infidelity itself. It's not the bad times in and of themselves that matter: it's how you respond to them. If you and your husband respond poorly to his affair, the chances of your marriage surviving diminish accordingly. You may respond well and take control of the situation, using it to help you grow. If you don't allow despair and feelings of anger and fear to win over your desire to use the affair as fertilizer to grow a marriage even stronger than the one you thought you had then your marriage stands an excellent chance of not just surviving but thriving. There's nothing like a fire to harden steel.

Chapter 3:
Facilitators of Cheating

The Cyberspace

Cyberspace is a major facilitator of infidelity. It takes only one click to find forbidden fruit online. There are countless websites where people can connect with no questions asked. Live intercourse of different styles is freely available and capable of compelling an undisciplined mind to try it out, especially when the partner at home is not performing as expected. The Internet is a major facilitator of cheating.

Avoiding Problems

Avoiding problems is the main contributor to infidelity. Giving excuses rather than facing the music with your partner opens the door to unfaithfulness, especially emotional affairs. Some people will tell you that they found a coworker or neighbor as a shoulder to lean on. This is why sympathetic coworkers or neighbors regularly become participants in infidelity.

We see porn actions

Pornography is widespread on the Internet, and it causes people to cheat on their partners. It absolutely leads to emotional affairs and the death of love and trust at home, where what you see is not provided by your partner. Porn addiction is a weighty factor causing the breakdown of relationships. Both sexes suffer from this problem. It is not discriminatory toward men. More and more ladies suffer from the Internet porn addiction today just as much as those rampaging men.

Facebook

Facebook is also a major contributing factor to rising infidelity. You can encounter and connect with anyone online. Instances where people have reconnected with former school lovers and resumed dating all over again after years of being in a marriage relationship are countless. Facebook fantasy is a significant cause of infidelity today.

Monotony

Monotony can lead to an external affair. Many people fall into a tired routine in the bedroom. You must do something to keep your marriage fresh. Illicit sex could be possibly avoided if people took the time and commitment to communicate verbally, emotionally, and physically to keep things exciting. Some people look for outside excitement to escape monotony. It can be by testing and experimenting with other relationships or hanging out with different people.

Partners are growing apart

Lovers who don't grow apart are an endangered species. Infidelity could creep in if you and your spouse have different goals. You must prepare to ride off into the sunset together after the children are grown. Your spouse should be your best friend and true love.

Addiction and unhealthy excesses

Drugs and alcohol often go hand in hand with illicit affairs. A person's addiction to drugs or alcohol is not different from an addiction to pornography, food, or any other unhealthy excess.

Married for the wrong reasons

Some might not have married for the right reasons, and they have not become the "right" person for their spouse. Again, do you both have enough in common and share things mutually? If not, you will often look for that missing camaraderie in the arms of someone else elsewhere. That is infidelity.

A dearth of respect from your partner

Do you respect and treat your spouse well? Does your spouse respect and treat you well in return? Please, ego-stroking leads to external affairs. Everybody enjoys a compliment and some respect; it would go a long way if spouses found ways to respect and complement each other frequently. A lack of respect will push a person to look for it elsewhere, and external affairs may result.

Lack of appreciation

Some partners fall into external affairs simply because they feel they are not treasured at home or are "doing all of the work alone" in keeping the marriage relationship and home life together. On the contrary, one must ask, am I appreciative of my partner? Am I the "right lover" for my partner? If we have a "servant's" mindset for our partner, cheating could be avoided.

Body image and ageing issues

Problems involving body structure, image, weight gain or loss, as well as aging, unfortunately, can cause cheating. Some partners will "trade-in" an aging lover for a "younger" one. The wedding ceremony is the beginning. Keep things fresh and continue chasing your partner for life to avoid infidelity.

Lack of confidence

A lack of confidence causes infidelity in a marriage. The need for continuous reaffirmation can lead to it, especially if one partner becomes "too needy" or "too insecure." This is a delicate balance to achieve, but the marriage relationship requires nothing less than true, honest ,and dedicated commitment.

The partners are residing in different cities

Work requirements that force a partner to travel a lot and live apart for long periods of time invariably leads to cheating. Avoid it and prioritize your partner.

Retaliation

Some partners won't forgive and let go if they discover that their partner has cheated on them. They will go ahead and retaliate by paying heavily in cash and in kind. This is dangerous and shouldn't occur.

Self-exploration could be responsible

Partners in happy relationships sometimes consider external affairs to be a liberal exploration of their sexuality. It might not have anything to do with the partner or marriage. The specific reason why happy partners cheat might vary from one person to another, but generally, self-exploration is often the root cause even if people don't understand it at the time. Most cheaters say they don't know why they are cheating on their partner. However, after delving into their pasts, it becomes clear why. They are searching for a brand-new version of themselves; it could be the one they once had and lost or were never able to find from birth.

The concept of marriage is modified

The concept of marriage is not what it used to be. In the past, marriage was about commitment, economic stability, and reproducing rather than finding lifelong love with a partner. Nowadays, partners expect all that and more. Consequently, if infidelity does occur, it's often the biggest betrayal possible in a marriage because there was so much packed into one relationship. Also, in this modern day, although we have the capacity to pick our partners and fall in love, infidelity still exists. Because of that, it has become something so destroying that many marriage relationships don't last once the infidelity happens.

Self-discovery

Related to self-exploration, some partners are enjoying their marriage but want to self-discover themselves by intentionally participating in illicit sex. There was a case involving a lady. She had a seemingly perfect, great life, and it hadn't always been that way. She did not let loose as a kid or had ever explored her sexual options. She got married young and worked full time to support her loving family. Her family was united and growing, but something was still missing. Eventually, she cheated with a guy she would never contemplate as a life partner, merely because she wanted to discover another option or version of herself.

Differing Responses of Men and Women

I will begin with a few statistics about men and women regarding infidelity and its consequences. Men are usually considered as the ones who cheat more, but is that really true? New research has revealed surprising facts about infidelity. Recent statistics show that more than one-half of men cheat on their partners, exactly 57 percent. But women are not far behind; 54 percent admit to infidelity.

Interestingly, they are more likely to seek a divorce than men. About 71 percent of divorces are initiated by women. Also, 53 percent of marriages end in divorce. Otherwise, 69 percent of women admitted they had chosen to be unfaithful because they no longer received any gifts from their partner, precisely the kind of attention that makes women feel valued and loved.

Healing from infidelity

Cheating results in a loss of trust, and it is not a behavior that is unique to only one sex. Both men and women cheat. At this time, we will focus on the woman's perspective, but that does not mean that men cannot learn something valuable by reading this. If I tell you this story from the perspective of both men and women, you will not understand it well. Instead, we will focus on one gender so you will understand it better.

There is a big difference in cheating and the actual definition of infidelity; it seems that different people come to different conclusions on the subject. For some, infidelity is the physical act of engaging in sexual relations with other people. Anything short of that does not count as cheating, at least not for them. Other people consider infidelity as romantic physical contact, which should only be reserved for one's partner, even if it does not include sexual intercourse.

Some believe that infidelity can exist even if there is no physical contact. If two people share something personal and intimate that would ordinarily be reserved only for one's partner, that is also infidelity. The fact is, if your partner is convinced that you have cheated because of the time, attention, or attachment you have given to another person, it constitutes infidelity in their mind.

Your relationship should be the most important thing in the world to you and, yes, friendships are wonderful, but if they impair intimacy and connection with your partner, then you are guilty of infidelity. That is a simple fact. Relationships should be built on trust and mutual respect. When you are the "other woman" how can you trust a person who cheats on your partner with you? If he cheats with you, do you have enough ego and vanity to believe that he won't cheat on you too?

One thing the psychologist knows about cheating that the public ignores is that cheating never happens because of the quality of the relationship. It is not because the partner or spouse was not good enough. Cheating happens because something is wrong with the person who is cheating.

There is no excuse that justifies infidelity. If the relationship is in trouble, then work on the problems. If you find that the relationship cannot be rescued, then break it. Do it with divorce if you are married or by leaving your partner if it's a relationship. Do this before you go looking for someone else. Just don't cheat! Cheating can never be justified and is never acceptable.

One thing that is as bad as cheating is the enabler of the cheater. Of course, that doesn't hold true if the person doesn't know that their lover is in a relationship. In such a case, the man should take full responsibility and face the consequences of his actions.

But if the other person is aware of the situation and chooses to continue the affair with the married man, then she is no better. It might be said that this other woman's infidelity is more unforgivable than his because, as a woman, she should understand how much infidelity hurts. She should never have entered into an affair at all.

As you look at the facts, bear in mind that the problem of infidelity is not the relationship, but it is the one who committed the infidelity. Then you will understand that the other woman can never be sure that she will not be deceived as well.

Once a cheater, always a cheater. If he is cheating, let him seek help. If it cheats again, you should just leave. But what do you do when you're with a cheater and know he's cheated on other women before you? The truth is that a man who has a past of cheating cannot be trusted in a relationship.

And if you are the "other woman", ask yourself something. Knowing his unfaithful history, what do you think it will be like to become the cheated one and learn that he has moved on to another? Of course, you think that things will be different with you. You will be everything he needs, but you are wrong.

There is nothing you can do, give, or become that will prevent a cheater from embarking on his "adventures". Cheating is cheating, both emotionally and physically, and if you allow it to continue, you are as guilty as the perpetrator. Don't worry; the time will come when, one day, he decides to move on to someone else, leaving you heartbroken just like the heart you helped him break when you participated in and encouraged his infidelity.

Not all men are cheats. Some are truly loving, willing to give anything to their partner and remain loyal to the end. This is the type of man you need to look for, instead of constantly trying to fix an irreparable cheat who will only break your heart and the hearts of other women.

If your man comes directly to you from the arms of another woman, you should flee because it will soon be your turn. If you don't, well, you've earned you everything it will do to your heart and your soul. Cheaters never win. Be honest with your partner, and if you prefer to be with someone else, end the relationship immediately.

If you are the "other woman," you must also end the affair immediately. That is the right thing to do, or one day you will be in the place of this devil's wife, but unlike his ex-partner, you will deserve every second of suffering.

Infidelity is a major social issue, and I will not clarify or classify the specific reasons. It is like the "golden rule". The truth is that the cheater has no scruples, and they do things the wrong way. Both men and women are the same. And there are no excuses.

There is the school of thought that if a woman cheats, she is signaling the end of her primary relationship, unlike a man. A woman cheats for different reasons compared to a man, and the idea holds a lot of weight. Men and women see relationships and sex differently. For men, it is easy to segment love and sex. For them, intimate connections and sex are different things. It is more like sex is sex, and relationships are relationships, and the two hardly overlap. Consequently, a man will cheat casually without easily feeling one degree of emotion, although it is not always the case. On the other hand, a woman will cheat differently where sex and intimacy are entangled, so compatibilization is more difficult.

Simply put, when a woman cheats, there is a degree of intimacy, romance, connection, or love. For men, cheating can be simply a way of fulfilling sexual urges and fantasies that are not met in the primary relationship. Of course, a good number of men cheat both emotionally and sexually because they are attracted to the outside partner, and many more do not. Infidelity for men can be just an opportunistic and primarily sexual activity that does not affect the main relationship. A large number of men report that they are happy in their primary relationship although they are cheating. Despite cheating, most men who have an affair have no intention of putting their primary relationship to an end.

Women, on the other hand, are less likely to separate love and sex. For the majority of them, sex and a bit of relational intimacy go together. More often than not, an intimate relation is more important than sex for women. That is why women are less likely to cheat unless they feel unhappy in their primary relationship or they are intimately connected with the partner they are cheating with. Either of these two reasons can make a woman leave the primary relationship.

A search was conducted where women and men were shown videos of people having sex: two men having sex, two women having sex, and man-woman sex. Most men were turned on by the video of a man and a woman and also woman-to-woman. Gay men were turned on only by the man-to-man sex. On the other hand, two-thirds of women were turned on by videos where there was an emotional and psychological connection regardless of gender. Numerous researchers have revealed that generally speaking, women are turned on by and attracted to emotional intimacy rather than physical intimacy. On the other hand, men are turned on by sex acts whether or not there are shown in committed relationships.

Male sexual desire is driven by physiological factors more than psychological ones. That explains why porn sites designed for men focus so much on overt sexual acts and body parts without adding many hints of emotions. Even porn literature designed for men focuses on sexual acts and not relationships and feelings.

When you tune in on shows and books written for women, you will see that the attention is on the flow of romance, love, relationship, and a happy ever after ending. You will find very little non-relational and objectified sex in shows designed for female consumers. Instead, you will see more love-at-first-sight, hearts melting, a story of two people in a long-term commitment, and heroes. Think of the **Fifty Shades of Grey** movie where the bad boy meets the good girl.

Typically, men do not need love to enjoy sex. They hardly need to like the person; all they want is a turn on, and they are good to go. It is harder to convince a woman to have sex because she will want a considerate man, who wants a home and children, has a sense of humor, is caring and sweet, and a lot of other related stuff.

Some researchers and therapists say that the complication for women when it comes to relationships is the result of years of experience. Let's take a look at this: when a woman is considering having sex with a man, her subconscious mind is looking at the long-term results. In the unconscious human software, the woman is aware that sex can alter her life forever. The possible results include pregnancy, nursing, and a life of raising children. Such a commitment would require resources, time, and enormous amounts of energy. As such, sex with the wrong guy can have devastating results.

Consequently, a woman tends to vet a possible mating partner thoroughly before any physical and psychological engagement or even getting intimate. Women have a safety mechanism hardwired in their minds, and they will not give in to sex until certain conditions are met. Surprisingly, women with histories of sexual trauma will have a weaker self-defense mechanism and consequently, they are more likely to cheat and become victimized as adults.

Men face fewer dangers when engaging in sex. Therefore, they have not identified the need to guard themselves and develop an inner detector. That is why men are likely to cheat even when they are in a happy relationship.

Chapter 4:
Psychology of Cheating

Infidelity affects everyone differently, and the psychology of cheating has been studied extensively. Taking a closer look at how perspective changes allows us to better understand the subject as a whole.

Why Do Men Cheat?

When we compare the biological differences between men and women, while taking emotion and personality out of the equation, we are given some vital clues as to why men may choose to cheat. When you compare men to heterosexual women, anatomy paints a clear picture. Men are more able to bounce around sexually than women.

Men are built to spread their seed. Women who menstruate are capable of having children. This means there will always be an inherent risk involved in general unless childrearing is the end-goal. Choosing to sleep with multiple partners increases the risk of becoming pregnant substantially.

Men take on significantly less risk, even when engaging with multiple partners. The slate is already cleared. If a male is predisposed or desires to find another mate, they are free to do so with little consequence. This may account for the fact that men are statistically more likely to cheat on their partners than women.

Some of the most reliable data we can find about men's motivations and the reasons they cheat come from psychiatrists' observations. The unfortunate truth is that no one wants to admit to being unfaithful. These individuals are already willing to misrepresent themselves. Statistical data is useful but is not completely accurate on this subject.

Psychiatrists suggest that from a male perspective, cheating can occur for many reasons. Dissatisfaction with one's current relationship was often noted. Some individuals wish to terminate their existing bond but are unsure how to end things with their partner.

Unfaithfulness rather than sincere communication places the onus on the slighted party. They want to be caught so the relationship will end, or at least they don't mind risking being found out. Some individuals engage in this behavior because they would like to break up but don't want to be alone. Cheating offers these persons the ability to move from one mate to another without ever being single.

This is another instance in which the unfaithful half of the relationship is aiming to be discovered. He actively wants his significant other to notice and be hurt by his betrayal. When one party in a couple is driven to betrayal based on a feeling of rage, it can cause some damaging effects outside of the obvious. The entire relationship becomes restructured around who can potentially do the most harm. A competition is started between the warring partners. Professional intervention is often required in these cases.

Situational infidelity is also quite common among both men and women, even in individuals who have never thought of being unfaithful before. It is natural to be attracted to others, even when you are in a happy and healthy relationship. These attractions only become dangerous when they are explored.

As mentioned, if you understand yourself to have feelings or budding sexual desire toward a friend, coworkers, etc., you should keep your distance from this person until the feelings are vanquished. Men have mentioned succumbing to their impulses when left alone with the object of their affection. This situation look as though a storm had just emerged from nowhere to destroy everything.

Even in these situations, professional help may ease the couple's burden. Poor impulse control is a marker that someone is more likely to cheat. It is also a characteristic that can be overcome.

Unresolved trauma can also be a factor in men's motivations to seek a new partner outside the relationship. Sometimes the pain has not even made itself known to the perpetrator; they simply feel drawn to destroying their relationship. These individuals use sex with strangers as a sort of drug. It provides an escape from the emotions and thoughts their connection to the existing partner might be exacerbating.

As a society, we tend to stigmatize men's emotional pain. Scars can be very real, and they can influence behavior that would otherwise be out of character. Some men are left trying to cope with an inability to form permanent bonds or properly attach to others romantically. Childhood abuse is at the root of many of these cases. Their distrust of romance has been hardwired into their brains through the actions of someone from their past.

These wounds must be worked through in therapy. The deeper and more complicated the pain, the more the couple would benefit from a professional's advice. Trying to resolve these old traumas on your own can be frustrating and even fruitless.

Inherently selfish tendencies can also play into a man's willingness to cheat. Regardless of gender or how the person identifies themselves, some individuals feel as though they are entitled to attention from others. These individuals may even be proud of their indiscretions.

This partner is probably not intentionally trying to cause pain. They just view the suffering of the faithful party as worth the risk of having fun. Men in this category tend to see affairs as challenges. They enjoy the sensual thrill of juggling multiple partners at once.

The risk of being discovered allows these men to feel alive. They want to exist beneath a tiny bit of peril, and they want the secrets that go along with having hidden lovers. These men will often attempt to justify their actions because they perceive themselves as being correct.

Men who act out of a purely selfish intent were frequently never interested in monogamy. These individuals tell their partners that they are going to remain faithful purely because that is what they felt was required to enter into the relationship. The relationship and their affairs are all puzzles to be completed for fun.

People who manipulate others for their own gain with no remorse are displaying narcissistic tendencies. They are likely to be emotionally abusive if nothing else. These individuals are always willing to find loopholes, just large enough to crawl through.

In the same family of intent, some men view themselves as better or more intelligent than the rest of the population. He will convince himself that he deserves to have another partner and affection from multiple sources.

These men see themselves as the plucky hero in their own stories. They suffer from delusions of grandeur and an inflated sense of self. The current partner is seen as inadequate, and he must seek the love of a stranger. He deserves this attention because he is inexplicably better than everyone around him.

Some men have set their standards incredibly high. So high that no reasonable partner would ever be willing or able to meet the ridiculous demands. This man believes that he deserves the absolute best and that his partner must wait on him like a servant. He expects the other half of the relationship to be ready, willing, and able to please him.

This individual has no understanding of the priorities of others. He runs over his partner's life and their needs with no hesitation. There is no one capable of living up to his standards, and when his current partner inevitably fails, he goes out searching for new attention.

Long-lasting love is formed within a couple when they have weathered the challenges of time. Their bond is more powerful and more lasting than infatuation. Some men cheat because they miss the feeling of fresh love. There is almost a chemical high associated with the level of passion and intensity between two new lovers.

This is a temporary feeling, though. It is easily chased away at a moment's notice. Men who find themselves chasing this sensation are leading a life of transience. That buzzy and intoxicating attraction is always going to sober into a more measured, nurturing bond.

Some men admit to having cut off their friends when they entered into their newest relationship. This can cause issues because now the significant other is placed in the role of being every friend. When the faithful partner in these couples fails to meet their significant other's expectations, they are cheated on.

In a healthy relationship, both parties have friends. They have their own priorities. No one has to change a great deal about themselves fundamentally. In healthy relationships, each participant can be trusted to go and make friends without the experience turning into a temptation.

The consumption of drugs and alcohol is already an indicator that individuals might be inclined to stray.

Men are also stereotypically able to compartmentalize sex. We often view men as less sentimental than women. Some therapists note that cheating men were unaware of the damage that their actions would cause to their relationship. These men believed that the actions they were engaging in were purely physical; *it's just sex*. They believe they are vindicated by the fact that they are a good partner in every other way.

These individuals do not understand the devastation that infidelity causes. This could account for the skew in statistics as twenty percent of men have been unfaithful at some point. Thirteen percent of women admit to having cheated.

There seems to be a common theme among the reasons that men have reported for cheating on their partners. Each justification echoes the sentiment that something was missing from the existing pair-bond. This is not an indictment of their partners, as there is no good excuse to betray a mate's trust.

Sometimes the missing piece is that the partner feels entitled to more time, sex, or attention than they are currently receiving. Other instances illustrate that the unfaithful party is merely looking to increase their body count, and they are missing the thrill of casual sex.

Why Do Women Cheat?

We need to examine both sides of the equation. Motivations between men and women run parallel in some ways, diverging in others. Men and women have a different brain chemistry and different lived experiences that weigh upon their choices. Neither gender is more benevolent than the other; they are merely operating from two separate places.

There are many commonalities that speak to positions and views that are inherently human and have nothing to do with gender. For instance, women have also reported cheating out of revenge toward their partner. They use the betrayal as a retaliation tactic, which can potentially ignite a blood-feud within the partnership.

Women have also mentioned engaging in infidelity due to a lack of sex in their existing relationships. This is another thing they have in common with men. They feel they are entitled to more attention and affection than they are receiving at home with their mate.

Building upon this attempted justification, some women are willing to cheat when they perceive a lack of emotional bonding in the existing relationship. In effect, she feels as though the connection has fizzled out. She needs to find another partner to allow herself the attention and affection she had been looking for.

Like their male counterparts, women sometimes engage in affairs when they wish the current relationship to end. This is a round-about method of avoiding communication. These individuals want to be caught so they have an excuse to end the partnership.

Individuals cheat when the relationship is dying because they are hoping to force their partner's hand. Breaking up is an uncomfortable and tedious process. Some women seek to circumvent the hard conversations by engaging in deal-breaking acts that cause their partner to take on an active role in the pair bond's dissolution.

Sex addiction causes infidelity in both men and women. It often indicates that an individual suffers from poor impulse control, but sometimes the addiction result from childhood trauma. No matter the cause, the result is the same.

Some women take addiction a step further by falling in love with the process of falling in love. These individuals crave the attention that comes with new relationships. The honeymoon phase is technically their drug.

They cheat on their existing partners in search of a new bond so they can experience the excitement and thrill that comes from a new romance. Again, this is not an indictment of the current partner. The tendency speaks to a deep flaw within the cheater that will likely have to be addressed with a professional.

Women with low confidence also seek out new mates. They are seeking validation through the eyes of another. These individuals may be depressed or anxious. Sex with an outside party allows these women to feel attractive and needed. Men have a similar tendency.

We have all watched television shows where the wife of a rich and busy man ends up sleeping with a member of the household staff. The portrayal is often overdramatic and silly, but it speaks to a deep truth. Some women engage in infidelity when they feel as though they are not being appreciated.

Perhaps their significant other has been spending more time at the office or has not being complimentary enough. Maybe their sex life has fizzled out or has not received the attention to which she feels entitled. Countless women have reported seeking a partner outside of the relationship due to feelings of inadequacy.

There has been a rise in the number of women who are bored in their relationships and marriages. They are resentful of the amount of maintenance they must do to keep the household functioning. The anger and boredom build until they find themselves pursuing a new partner. These individuals find themselves being weighed down by the expectations of domestic life. Some women have stated that the affair allows them to maintain their existing marriage.

Just like their male counterparts, some women have been reported turning to affairs because their expectations are too high. Their existing relationship partner is expected to fulfill all their needs, all of the time. They are not allowed to have lives of their own. These women feel entitled to attention and affection constantly.

When her partner cannot meet their ridiculous expectations, the woman (in this scenario) turns to infidelity. She attempts to supplement the things she feels she needs. These individuals feel justified in their actions. They believe that the partner's inability to satisfy their every desire is a punishable offense.

Women may also find themselves in situations that encourage cheating, just like the men described above. We will discover that all across the board, it is a bad idea to place yourself in situations where you have the opportunity to bond with someone you are already attracted to.

Admitting it

Coming clean to your partner can take an outrageous amount of courage. The truth is a decisive first step within the process of healing. Your spouse or partner will be upset, but the situation will improve in the long run. If you wish to stay with your partner, this is a necessary first step.

Bring this information to the table sooner rather than later. The longer you wait, the more damage the truth will cause. Infidelity is a betrayal, and when the faithful partner is lied to for an extended period of time, it can be even more devastating. Hiding the truth makes your significant other feel stupid or embarrassed.

Plan to reveal this information in a private setting. Ensure there is enough time for both of you to be heard. The most important piece of this puzzle requires that you be respectful of their needs. This is an intense conversation so pick a day when you both have time to think and respond to one another.

Go into the conversation knowing that you might lose your relationship. Infidelity is a deal-breaking offense for so many people. Do your best to remain calm and explain yourself without pulling out inane excuses. Your honesty will be appreciated even if it isn't right at that moment.

Having this conversation with your partner takes a lot of bravery. You are not a bad person, but you must take accountability for your actions. If you intend to heal your relationship with your significant other, it will take some work. Enter the discussion with an open mind and an open heart.

Chapter 5:
Various Types of Infidelity

Before a new relationship commences, the partners must communicate with one another. These candid talks can be difficult to stomach, but they may be the key to safeguarding oneself against the emotional trauma that comes with rebuilding after an affair. Each individual's preferences should be laid upon the table.

We each have expectations for our partners. There are lists of behaviors we would deem inappropriate within the confines of healthy relationship. Our boundaries must be made clear so they are not inadvertently stomped on.

Each individual perceives acts of infidelity through the lens of their own life experiences. Events can occur that potentially color the way we think about cheating. These predispositions should be shared with a potential partner so that both parties can better navigate the relationship.

Physical cheating

Physical cheating is well known and universally feared. This behavior includes physical touch or contact. It usually includes a period of building tension that explodes into an affair, but it can also occur situationally.

Physical cheating usually occurs in the form of sexual engagement with an individual other than one's own partner. It can be especially damaging for the faithful half of the relationship, regardless if the act was planned or spontaneous. Don't hesitate to discuss your personal parameters for this type of infidelity.

Men are more interested in this type of affair. They both fear their partners entering into a physical affair, and they, themselves, have been involved in physical affairs. Women show an affinity for emotional affairs.

Micro-cheating

This is the love child of physical and emotional infidelity. Imagine you have difficulty talking with your partner. You have disclosed all of the ways you have been hurt and outlined the behavior you wish your significant other to avoid.

Micro-cheating occurs when your partner knowingly is balanced upon the line of what is acceptable to you. This behavior is an attempt to get as close to actual contact as possible without having to deal with the negative consequences of traditional infidelity. If your partner seems to be encouraging a playdate with fire, they could be engaging in this brand.

The inherent damage associated with micro-cheating comes from sneaking around. There is a level of dishonesty. The offending partner may not be seeing or sleeping with another person, but the lying will cause a similar amount of destruction.

Every relationship is founded upon an agreement. Micro-cheating is a betrayal of that agreement and has the potential to shatter the trust of the faithful partner. The perpetrator knows that their balancing act will hurt their significant other, or there will be no measure to hide their actions. By hiding, the cheater has communicated that they have weighed their options and decided to pick something fun over their companion's feelings. This will cause a fissure.

Some psychologists believe that we hold partners to a too high standard. Human beings are naturally attracted to new faces outside of their existing relationships. These individuals believe that strict and uncommunicated rules set for significant others are unfair. It fosters a partnership built on impossible expectations. Even if this view is correct, damage can be mitigated by sharing and discussing boundaries before the relationship begins.

Emotional Cheating

This is a buzzword repeated in every conversation surrounding infidelity. This is a creeping and insidious form of betrayal characterized by establishing a non-physical, romantic relationship behind the partner's back. The offending party will often try to justify these indiscretions as touch was not initiated.

Emotional cheating is widely regarded for the devastation it can cause when inflicted upon healthy relationships. The unfaithful partner often connects to an individual outside of the relationship while simultaneously disconnecting from their own significant other. The establishment of bonds with another is the gateway to physical cheating that is known to escalate into affairs.

It is perfectly reasonable to expect that your significant other will form friendships with individuals of the sex they are attracted to. Emotional cheating creates such a blurred line because it is often conflated with platonic friendship. Picking up on problematic behaviors can be difficult and may leave the faithful partner feeling suspicious and silly. The development of feelings should be heeded and immediately smothered to avoid potentially engaging in emotional cheating.

The following are signs that indicate emotional cheating:

- A partner beginning to lie about their connection with an outside party can be a red flag. The unfaithful party will seek to understate their bond to the new individual.

- Emotional cheaters tend to complain about their current partner with the outside individual. This occurs to send the signal to the "friend" that their existing relationship is unstable.

- Excessive hugging or touching toward someone outside of the relationship. Looking for any excuse to be close to or engage in touch is a sign that an attraction has developed.

- Hiding or deleting phone calls and texts can signal that one partner is engaging in conversations that would make their significant other uncomfortable.

If you suspect your partner has become entangled in one of these attachments, it is best to place the outside friendship on pause. Have an open and honest conversation with your significant other. It can help to outline expectations going forward. If you are currently dealing with a situation of this nature, it can be prudent to take a step back from the relationship.

Technology and Cheating

The steady advancement of technology has made the prospect of finding a partner outside of the relationship more convenient than ever. Emotional cheating is especially easy and facilitated through social media platforms. The physical distance can virtually eliminate the guilt the offending party suffers typically.

People can log onto a website with the intention of finding a companion. Within moments one could find oneself engaged in conversation with a stranger. These exchanges can become deeply personal, romantic, or sexual in nature.

Spilling one's heart to someone through a screen can be much more comfortable than doing so in real life. It seems as though a void is being filled. These are the reasons that unfaithful partners are tempted to form bonds with strangers online.

Some apps can be used to maintain the user's anonymity. Other applications delete the file that was sent, so there is no trace of correspondence. These programs can be used to hide communications efficiently.

Although it's not easy to accept, cheaters are not bad people. They have made mistakes, but those mistakes do not have to define the individual. The damage that occurs as a result of online cheating is devastating. Guilt is somewhat removed from the equation, making it much easier to offend.

The faithful parties in these relationships suffer. They are left with a visual representation of their significant other's infidelity. There are logs and messages saved upon devices. The betrayed partner will dig through all of the available communication while comparing themselves to the recipient. It is the nature of the innocent party to blame themselves for the actions of the wandering partner.

They are forced to gaze upon the interactions in which their partner indulged. The entirety of the outside relationship is available to be read and scrutinized. This aspect of the affair usually is missing from physical Infidelity.

The faithful partner is also left with the knowledge that their significant other cheated over a device -a device we all carry around all the time. There is unlimited access, which instills a paranoia that the infidelity will happen again and again.

Risk Factors

Infidelity is the leading cause of the dissolution of relationships. Affairs are not an uncommon problem. If you find yourself in a partnership where you suspect your significant other is cheating, know you are not alone. Should you find yourself on the wrong end of an affair, know that this happens quite a bit - and always has.

Partners who become caught up in affairs are not inherently evil. Sometimes poor decision making can be an indication that the individual needs help. Some people find themselves lashing out in cruel ways to mask their own need for assistance.

Narcissistic personality types are more likely to cheat on their partners, but that does not mean that every person who has been involved in an affair is narcissistic. No set type of personality indicates that a person will stray. There are, however, traits that suggest someone is more likely to engage in the behavior.

Intellectual curiosity, an otherwise remarkable trait, means that an individual is more likely to seek out a partner outside of their relationship. Of course, this doesn't mean that any curious person is suddenly a danger to their significant other. Look for a combination of factors when there are already clues that an affair is occurring or might occur soon.

Intellectual curiosity is a character trait that finds its home in those always looking for adventures and new experiences. An affinity for the arts and various other creative pursuits can indicate that an individual is in possession of this trait. These people will express an impressive imagination.

Impulsiveness can be a precursor for all sorts of detrimental behaviors. These individuals have a difficult time pumping the breaks when it comes to their personal desires. Being impulsive can make someone fun or spontaneous; the darker side to these tendencies is that they will not always act in your or their own best interest.

There has been evidence linking these personality traits to hormones that make an individual more likely to cheat on their partner. Impulsive people have a difficult time saying "no" to any new challenge. They also lack the will power that would naturally prevent them from making bad judgment calls.

Disorganized individuals are, unfortunately, also on the chopping block. This trait can indicate a lack of self-control. Those who score low with conscientiousness are also more prone to fall into this category. This trait could mean that an individual is distractible.

Outgoing partners can attract the attention of others. These individuals also crave a certain amount of acknowledgement, potentially leading them to stray from the relationship's confines. They assert themselves when the situation requires it of them. These people have a lot of friends and may even be flirty by nature.

Competitiveness can signal that someone is more likely to cheat. These individuals are stubborn and can potentially appear rude. They do not work well with other people, and they value having someone to best. They are always striving to have the most valuable car or the most attractive mate. They also enjoy the thrill of chasing a potential partner. Anything that can be gamified is going to be more attractive to some competitive people.

Sexual Risk-Taking is often associated with partners who might eventually become open to finding sexual gratification outside the existing relationship. If you or your partner find yourself more prone to seek out escalating measures for seeking excitement within the bedroom, this could potentially be a warning sign. Being open to trying new things does not automatically make an individual a cheater, but it could be a tendency to keep a watchful eye on.

Pornography has also been linked to a willingness to seek a partner outside of the relationship. It encourages the consumer to form unrealistic standards concerning sex. When these standards are unable to be met, they venture outside of the relationship.

Nervous people can be depressed, anxious, or withdrawn. Sometimes these individuals are dealing with personal trauma. These individuals may also have an issue with anger. They feel as though they are vulnerable to the outside world.

Chapter 6:
How to Avoid Divorce due to Infidelity

Must I divorce my cheating husband? Is breaking up or leaving a solution if my wife/husband cheating? Should I forgive and forget or separate from my husband/wife for their infidelity? Can our marriage be saved still after a betrayal? When must I walk away after being betrayed? Is it fine to divorce a cheating partner if you still love them? These are just a few of thousands of questions you bear in mind if you find your partner is cheating.

To answer them, it's important to ask yourself even more questions and determine what cheating and being unfaithful means to you exactly. Is it an emotional affair, a kiss, or sexual intercourse?

Divorce has a reputation for being bad, but what in specific terms does a divorce bring us that we so desperately want to avoid.

Loneliness

Divorce means that you and your once happy-to-be-together spouse are going your separate ways. You can no longer do things together, and any dreams you had in common are instantly buried. You are now going to be doing a lot of things separately, and this can quickly get very lonely. And when your divorce is fresh, it can make things hard to get through.

Children

The emotional and psychological trauma that children go through during a divorce is huge, and sometimes they get to go through it all on their own. In some societies, these children quickly feel stigmatized and that they are different from most people around them. They also suffer from divided loyalty and being clueless about how to handle it. If not properly managed, divorce can have a lasting impact on children and on their outlook on love and life well into their adult years.

Health degeneration

When the divorce is nasty, you have to take extra care to look after your health. Divorce can easily lead to depression and contemplation of suicide. You have to make sure you are emotionally stable so you do not have health issues to deal with.

You have to change your friends

Divorce forces you to rearrange your personal life. While you are trying to move on, you will need to change your friends and the people you mingle with. You will need to avoid the friends that you and your spouse once shared and begin to find new ones. Getting divorced means that you have to start building a social life that has no connection with your spouse.

Financial contribution to the divorce process

Divorce is an expensive undertaking. It can drain your finances. Hiring an attorney or an arbitrator will cost you some personal funds. After your divorce, you might want to begin thinking about rebuilding your finances.

Divorce Statistics after Infidelity

Is there a strong correlation between infidelity and divorce? Marriage after infidelity statistics provide that approximately 62% of spouses claim they would leave their partner after cheating while 31% would not consider it a problem. At the same time, further research reveals that 60-75% of marriages continue after an affair. So the question is, how many marriages end up in divorce after adultery?

Adultery is still the leading issue that ends up in divorce. In fact, in a study, 88% of spouses claimed that cheating was the main factor in divorcing their partner. What's interesting here is that only one of the partners considered adultery a problem, while the other one simply doesn't value what being loyal is.

How Does Adultery Affect a Divorce?

Adultery can ruin even the best of relationships, so it's essential to deal with the issue as soon as possible, or it can escalate the existing marital problems even more. However, before you make an important decision that will impact your family, it is important to take into account the traps and pitfalls that lead to cheating before you blame your partner for being unfaithful. You have to consider all the essential factors before you end your marriage.

People are prone to going to extremes while analyzing the situation that led to adultery. Some become too emotional and can't think straight, while others take into consideration only the rational reasons, trying to be objective, but they neglect their feelings as a result. In short, it is all connected to psychology. Remember, there are no right or wrong feelings, so don't judge yourself for your irrational emotions.

How to Decide Whether You Should Stay

Trust Your Gut

If you are the kind of person who doesn't tolerate infidelity, it would be hard to convince yourself that you are capable of forgiving your partner. However, if you still feel attached to the person, it may be possible to fix the issue. It is crucial to decide if you should divorce your husband or wife for cheating. Remember, no stereotypes or social norms should guide you. Trust your gut to understand what you truly need and see a therapist.

Avoid Taking Revenge

When to walk away after infidelity? Does revenge precede the final breakup? Some people indulge in revenge sex after their partner has cheated on them. This is inevitably a very bad idea because such behavior might cause even more suffering as a result.

If you want to have revenge sex because you feel hurt, then think again. This happens because it's impossible to compensate for the pain with more pain. Sex with someone else in any form is unlikely to restore a failing marriage. On the contrary, it will probably make rebuilding trust twice as hard. Thus, dealing with anger after infidelity is essential to avoid more costly mistakes.

Forgive Yet Never Forget

Many people can't tell the difference between forgiving and forgetting while understanding it is essential to heal from the wounds caused by infidelity. Mature people are able to forgive, but they still acknowledge the infidelity. After all, you never know where life will bring you, so it is best to mind those red flags rather than sending them to sweet oblivion.

True forgiveness isn't easy; you have to accept your resentment, deal with it, and let it go to finally experience relief and be able to communicate with your partner as usual. After all, it will allow you to heal your inner world, regain self-respect, and make more conscious decisions.

Compassion is what makes it possible to forgive another person. Mutual empathy is the most critical factor in maintaining a state of forgiveness. Understanding the errors of the other person makes it easy to forgive and turns feelings of revenge and anger into empathy. The role played by both partners in a relationship with infidelity issues should revolve the rebuilding process with the intention of seeking and granting forgiveness. The willingness of one partner to forgive depends on the honesty of the other. The betrayed partner needs to forgive themselves for being betrayed and forgive the other partners for the betrayal. The betraying partner needs to acknowledge their mistake and accept forgiveness humbly while showing gratitude. Through a subtle and careful process, the majority of couples forgive one another. They demonstrate that they have let go of the past. In an air of affection and sensitivity, they deal with the consequences of the affair together.

Carolyn overheard a group of women in church boasting about her husband, Chas. Carolyn was aware that it was not an unfounded rumor because she saw Rhonda flirting and making precise moves on Chas. When Carolyn told him, he put his arms around her and said, "I am sorry that you had to hear that disturbing gossip because of what I've done." Carolyn felt his repugnance was genuine, and she was comforted, as her main concern was to protect herself.

Some couples have formed symbolic rituals to mark the end of the affair and faithfulness as a new beginning. It is very important for the relationship. One suggestion by Gloria Harris is that the affair should come to an end by listing the wrongdoing done by both parties and throwing it into a river together. The combustion and burial of ashes of betrayal also symbolizes a funeral for the affair. Couples who believe they have failed in upholding their vows can choose to make new vows and promises to each other.

Many partners benefit from a more organized ritual in which forgiveness is officially sought and awarded for particular hurtful actions committed. When you hear specific apologies, you can decide to grant forgiveness. While one spouse is explicitly chosen to be the suspect and the other as the innocent victim, this strategy is suitable for couples ready to apologize and be forgiven by formal let-go procedures.

Childhood Impact on Committing Infidelity

What comes to mind is why do we stop communicating, especially when it's so critical? The answer is for myriad reasons, not the least of which is what got wired into us as kids.

Let me start with a fairytale since that's where a lot of misconceptions and fantasies begin, based on unrealistic expectations. The one I'm thinking of encapsulates the mating dance.

We hope that our significant others are mirrors that will reflect the best in us and not notice our uglier parts. Indeed, at first, the mirror, mirror on the wall, sees us as the fairest of all. But when that mirror shatters, we create our own bad luck; i.e., instead of making each other feel safe enough to be our authentic selves, we start to get critical of each other and go back to hiding our imperfections, only this time, there is no high to help us feel good like that initial rush.

As such, many people start to fear that their partner has changed somehow – or pulled a bait and switch – and they become disillusioned and start to lose interest. At that point, if they don't try to fix things, it can be just a matter of time before their eyes turn elsewhere, searching for the high of lust-driven infatuation.

A lot of this has to do with what our childhoods have taught us about relationships. So allow me to give you a synopsis of how our childhoods impact our adult relationships, which may explain betrayal wounds in a way that will help you understand why we stay or stray. It explains why some of us work through betrayals and come out stronger, while others fall to pieces and can never move past them. The same event can show different results in different people. Those who had caregivers who helped them out through tough moments know how to manage while those who had no one to help them or teach them how to cope remain forever stuck in their traumas, which can play out in horrific ways. This is a similar presentation to how Post Traumatic Stress Disorder develops.

Our childhoods mold our relationships for the rest of our lives; it's where our "attachment styles" develop, where we learn to enter into relationships, and where we can either feel safe or have our first brush with dysfunctionality. While it makes sense to want to repeat the good, what doesn't make sense is that we often end up repeating the bad as well.

Chapter 7:
Are Adultery and Infidelity the Same?

Many scholars who claim expertise in love and relationships believe that adultery and infidelity are two sides of the same coin but that claim is just wrong.

Where is the difference?

The difference between these two types of cheating is clear, and I honestly don't understand why some authors are claiming there is no difference. These so-called life coaches and self-proclaimed experts are perhaps attempting to erase the differences between adultery and infidelity to further liberal concepts. There is, however, a difference, and there is no point in denying that fact.

Similar behavior

Motivations for either kind of cheating are pretty much the same. They are related, so the cheater compensates with a selfish act that hurts their loved one. The hurt may be similar, but the difference between adultery and infidelity is significant. Read on to see how and why infidelity is much worse than adultery.

Adultery

I have asked many persons what adultery is. "Would you, and under what circumstances, forgive the adulterer?" I heard answers mostly from a moral perspective. I do believe that is the core of this whole story, which inevitably leads to the relativization of the act of adultery itself. Is adultery worse than infidelity, and more importantly, what is love and what does it have to do with adultery?

Since the words "love" and "deceit" are impossible to use precisely because they are in the academic realm of truth and error, the bottom line is to let everyone use them as they wish. Here I imply the existence of a parallel, secret relationship where the one who cheats voluntarily in their relationship/marriage is compared to the one who has committed themselves to faithfulness and love. Whether monogamy is a natural or an unnatural phenomenon is also a question as old as man. Let it be said that we have agreed that we will be monogamous because this is how we affirm our partnership.

Faithfulness

An important point to understand when it comes to relationships or marriage is that the point of it all is to stay together and grow old together, to relive those important moments, to share both happiness and sadness, to raise children and to always be there for one another, in good times and bad. The one important thing we often talk about I s faithfulness. When we enter into a relationship or marriage, it is our hope that the feelings of love we have for our partner encompass faithfulness. We expect that our mutual love will sustain a faithful relationship. Considering that both partners are adults and in a relationship/marriage they have chosen, the expectation of fidelity is only imposed. Being monogamous is a matter of choice, so no one can tell you that he is unfaithful because "it is in his nature". Remember that establishing an emotional balance actually helps us feel good about the relationship/marriage. However, the range of emotions is wide, so we often have conflicting emotions over which we have no control. At some level, we are likely not even aware of these emotions.

What is happening subconsciously?

When we are in a relationship/marriage that prevents us from engaging in loving relationships with other people, it is actually from the love we feel for our partner. While we may feel the desire to meet someone new, to have long and interesting conversations, to hold hands for the first time, to kiss for the first time, we come to the painful realization that life may have been different for us and our relationship/marriage is just one version of what we may have had - and only one version of the life we could have lived. Perhaps we could have lived a better life, and maybe we could have made better choices. However, in the end, we must accept that we have closed the door to all other choices, and this is the life we are living right now.

When we in a long relationship/marriage, it frequently happens that one of the partners feels neglected. The very act of neglect is one of the principal reasons why people cheat. Many think that cheating will result in jealousy and shift attention back to the neglected one. Therefore, do not neglect your partner; give them the love and support they need because it leads to mutual satisfaction and an environment that reduces the prospect of cheating.

It is crucial and vital to understand that we are not all the same. Some people are unable to express their dissatisfaction; they can't say no or confront insults. This is another reason for cheating. Some seek to punish their partner, only to feel a biting conscience afterward. However, avenging ourselves by cheating on our partners does not make us less angry or hurt. Cheating can even lead us to be even angrier and more hurt because our partners may show kindness to us.

But is it really so, or is it just a subjective feeling? After a while, the cheating person, however angry with their partner, begins to feel guilty. These emotions can be so intense that it begins to disrupt their lives. It becomes difficult to concentrate and carry out their routines and daily tasks. So ask yourself, is it worth it to go through this psychic torture? And when you blame and punish yourself, it is definitely the worst kind of torture because you will never be able to escape it alone.

My first tip is not to cheat, so you won't ever have to blame yourself. But if you've already cheated, my advice is to let it go. It's over, the damage has been done, and you need to find a way to forgive yourself.

Sometimes a relationship is burdened with the complicated subtext of "I hate you for loving you", or "I hate you for loving you so much", etc. Then the partners hurt each other just to see if the other can handle all of their issues. So, if they don't leave, then it's somehow proof of their love and dedication. Only when they fail to destroy themselves as a couple do they feel safe. Those are the words of an expert, but this compulsion to destroy out of love, for me, is rather weird and abnormal. This behavior is nothing less than masochistic.

Let's see what infidelity is.

Infidelity

Faithfulness is a virtue that is completely neglected today. There is little talk of fidelity. We all know what is physical betrayal. We all understand what physical violence is, but emotional violence receives little attention. An emotional being is invisible, yet is just as important as the physical being. Just as we wash our faces, so should we wash our emotional selves. It's one entity, made up of boundaries like a grid, a geographical map, or like the bloodstream—a coordinate system. If you have not paid the price of infidelity, you may declare that the one who asks you to pay violates your freedom; it means that you do not understand the limits. No—no one violated your freedom. You violated someone else's freedom because you knew where you were going and what the rules were.

So there are rules of the game. If you play chess, you can't use the rules used in "don't be mad, man." Someone will say, "But relationships are not a game." They are not a game; there is no intent to defeat an opponent, but they are the same in that both have rules, i.e., boundaries, and you both begin the relationship out of your own free will. When you've already entered into a relationship, then the question is whether you view the relationship as a team whose goal is the same, or do you view the relationship as an opportunity to defeat your partner. If we are speaking of close, emotional relationships, then we must agree that it is always a team game. So the goal is the same. The goal is love and peace.

Inside every being is the desire for peace. Every man seeks peace, tranquility and security. When you enter into an emotional relationship with someone, it is clear that the ultimate goal of that journey is peace. We can achieve peace if we strive for satisfaction and contentment. If we view relationships as boats propelled by rowing, then we will do our best to paddle so that the boat reaches its destination.

Treason, deceit and infidelity areas are akin to drilling a hole in your boat. Imagine two people paddling, and one drops the paddle and starts drilling a hole in the bottom of the boat. This is betrayal.

People portray betrayal and deception as the physical act itself. However, the physical act is only the manifestation of betrayal. If you know your inner self well, and if your partner knows your inner self and your boundaries, then it should be clear that enjoying long conversations with other people, thinking about others, and fantasizing is a form of betrayal.

The difference

We discussed the difference between adultery and infidelity. Adultery is more a natural urge, or lust if you will. Adultery does not include love, and that is the difference.

With infidelity, there are no clear reasons. Everything might be working well in the relationship, but for some people, that doesn't matter at all. They have their own set of rules; they don't have the proper values or a sense of morality.

That is why infidelity is the worst form of betrayal. But you need to know that you will be happy again. Do you now realize why you need to be strong and move on? Don't analyze your feelings and yourself. Don't close yourself off. There is a whole world around you. You will manage to build your life again with someone who deserves you.

Can infidelity be predicted?

There is no surefire method of discerning if your partner might seek out an affair. There is, however, one common factor that many cases of infidelity have in common. If your existing relationship is sick or in need of maintenance, then attending to those issues would be the most effective way to safeguard yourself against a potential intruder. The following are signs that your relationship could be in danger:

You and your partner are spending less and less time together. Neither of you is making room for one another. Couples tend to go through cycles of being affectionate and then keep their distance; however, if your significant other behaves excessively in their avoidance, it could mean something else is happening.

You spend most of your time on your cell phone, and your partner does the same. When the honeymoon period ends, it can be challenging to avoid phone habits. We are all guilty of using our phones in the evenings when we are looking to entertain ourselves after a long day. A relationship that is in trouble will see an even more dramatic uptick in time spent in the presence of another distraction. If you and your partner have stopped speaking regularly, this can be a warning.

Resentment is beginning to take over the relationship, and you find yourself snapping at your partner. Day-to-day life can wear on couples, but if you find yourself being increasingly annoyed with your partner or vice versa, this can be a sign that things are headed in the wrong direction.

You feel as though you are no longer a priority in your partner's eyes. Does your significant other still make time for you? Have you been taking a backseat to their friends or other engagements? This can be a sign that the relationship is becoming stagnant.

The other is spending more time than usual away from you.

They (or you) are sexually withdrawn. There are a good number of reasons for a change in sex-drive. You could feel self-conscious, or they could be stressed out. Sex slowing down in combination with other factors can be a sign that the relationship needs repair.

They are vague or evasive in their responses toward you. If they seem to be withholding information, this can indicate that they are becoming closed off.

What are signs that my partner is cheating?

While every person is different, some changes can help you determine if you should be concerned about a partner's behavior. Those who find themselves involved in infidelity are often left wracked with guilt. They grow more and more distant to the point that the relationship begins to change.

We will examine some of the signs that your partner is looking for something outside the relationship.

Your partner is cautious with their language, especially when speaking of their future plans. This is especially important if there has been a change and you are no longer being included in their musings.

You notice that they are focusing their online attention on one individual. They perhaps like the posts or pictures from only one person.

There are new lamentations about the lack of excitement in your life. Does your partner suddenly blame you for the complacency in the relationship? This can indicate a shift in thinking. If it seems as though your partner is suddenly focused more upon your flaws than before, this can be a warning sign.

Your significant other seems detached. Relationships are always going to change and become more comfortable and less intense; this is their usual lifecycle. However, if your partner is speaking to you significantly less, it could mean they are searching for validation elsewhere.

They have had affairs in the past. This is only relevant when combined with other items on this list.

Has your partner accused you of cheating? It's an old cliché, but it is a cliché for a reason. Cheaters often try to hide their actions by casting allegations on those close to them, including their significant others.

Your partner is protective of their phone. People are not secretive unless they have something to hide. There is a reason for evasive behavior. Watch to see if your significant other is using their device more than usual. If so, question their habits. If your partner is defensive or indignant in their response, then it could be worth investigating further.

Does your partner excessively mention one person from work or school? Have they recently stopped bringing this person up altogether? When we perceive our friendships as platonic, we wish to share. When one is aware that they have become romantic, the guilt causes silence.

Has your partner recently taken a renewed interest in the way they look? This can be a sign that they are trying to impress a new friend.

Does your significant other seem weirdly resentful? Affairs are emotionally involved beasts. Sometimes, the cheating partner becomes frustrated with the inability to remove themselves from the existing relationship.

None of these factors by themselves mean that your partner is absolutely engaging in infidelity. This list is merely a resource to help you discern when more attention should be paid to your partner's actions. It is only through observation and communication that we are offered the truth.

Cognitive Dissonance and Repeat Offenders

Infidelity is popularly understood to be a moral wrong. These views have not changed much as society has progressed, though attitudes are beginning to become more open surrounding the subject. You can look back at old folklore where infidelity was punished among the gods. In the second canonical book of the Christian bible (Exodus), you will find the phrase, "never commit adultery." This further leads to the belief that humankind has always been a mostly monogamous species.

Only about three percent of mammals are monogamous, and we fit firmly into that category even though extra-pair copulation is common in humans. We have already taken a look at the ambiguous biological evidence of our genetic coding. What else could contribute to pro-infidelity attitudes?

You have probably heard the term, cognitive dissonance, when discussing topics related to psychology. When taking a closer look at infidelity, it is easy to see where cognitive dissonance fits into the equation. This phenomenon is partially responsible for "once a cheater, always a cheater."

Cognitive dissonance is defined as holding contradictory beliefs (likely moral) around behavior. When we recognize an act as being damaging or hurtful to ourselves or others, and we participate in the act anyway, we engage in cognitive dissonance. Believing two contradicting ideas at the same time is uncomfortable.

Couples were surveyed on the topic of infidelity. They were asked how intensely wrong they believed the act of cheating to be, morally. Those who had never been unfaithful rated infidelity as being a severe offence.

Individuals who had cheated on their partners in the past had more relaxed views toward infidelity. This illustrates the uncomfortable nature of cognitive dissonance. These partners could not reconcile their actions with their belief that betraying a partner's trust was wrong, so they were forced to change their moral views on the matter. This could account for why some individuals engage in infidelity repeatedly.

Becoming a Cheater

Some people reading this book have cheated on partners in the past and are looking for insight into their own behavior. Some individuals never thought of engaging in an affair but are curious about the process. Those who have been slighted in their relationships can find a grain of catharsis in the examination of their partner's motives. The following is a very general estimation of the events surrounding the decision to cheat.

Finding yourself in an emotional affair is not exceedingly difficult if you are not actively guarding against it. These relationships begin as friendships. You meet someone at work, at school, or online. You and this individual hit it off, exchanging jokes and banter at first.

In the digital age, it can be easy to distract yourself from an existing relationship. Over time, all of the giddy and dreamy feelings you had for your long-term partner are shaped and molded into something else. Your relationship moves from flirty and fun to stable and comfortable. You are no longer expending effort to get ready for date night. The two of you are always involved in your own thing, sometimes forgetting to have conversations at all. These behaviors set the stage for an affair.

For the sake of the example, we will say that you met your new friend at work. You spend most of your shifts talking and laughing. You find yourself looking forward to the shifts you work together.

As time rolls on, you become closer and closer to the new friend. You are rationalizing this connection as being platonic. You find yourself beginning to disconnect even more from your existing partner. You two are so comfortable around one another that there is little in the way of newness or excitement.

You begin to speak to your work friend outside the job. Once this barrier is broken, the others fall with ease. The amount of time you spend communicating with this individual is growing. You spend many of your nights answering messages from your work friend. Likewise, they are also investing a lot of time getting to know you.

You find yourself thinking of this individual more and more. This is the moment when the mask begins to slip and you can finally see yourself in the mirror. You are attached to this individual. Interacting with your friend is similar to taking a drug because of the hormonal high the conversations give you.

The responsible action to take at this moment includes stepping away from your friend, creating distance between you and the person you are slowly beginning to realize you are attracted to. It is much easier to suggest putting this friendship on the back burner than it is actually to do so. These conversations are your only source of excitement throughout the long days, and you look forward to the interactions.

You continue talking to your friend. Slowly the conversations begin to turn. They do so little by little, in a way that you almost overlook. Soon you are exchanging flirty texts and then deleting them from the log in your phone. It is at this point that you have engaged in an emotional affair.

Allowing the situation to continue unchecked could easily lead to a physical and sexual affair. There are so many different situations that lead to infidelity. They are often approached with baby steps. A lot of grey-area decisions are made until you finally reflect upon your actions and realize what you have done.

Chapter 8:
Preventing the Reoccurrence of Infidelity

We all have witnessed some of our friends complete their lives flipped upside down because of infidelity. In today's society, it has become something a bit too shrugged off. Rates of divorce are on the rise because of it and it has become almost commonplace.

Your family doesn't have to become a victim of infidelity. Without the proper precautions, however, you leave your marriage vulnerable to the problem. Here are ways you can safeguard your marriage against infidelity while building a better relationship with your partner.

Avoid Temptation

The last thing that any marriage needs is one partner spending a lot of time around people who are tempting their desires. Maybe you have felt lustful for someone at work, for example. In this case, it's important to keep all contact strictly professional and avoid alone time with that person. Don't put yourself into a situation where things could go terribly wrong.

When you start allowing small things such as fantasizing about another person, it leads to bigger problems. You'll find yourself justifying cheating before you realize it. Before you see yourself in a tempting situation, it's best to avoid these situations completely. There's a big possibility that you are going to run into someone — an old flame from high school, a coworker, a hairstylist, a neighbor — that you find very sexy and attractive. Fair enough.

Simply keep yourself away from temptation if there's any risk of things getting too hot to handle, Avoid the person and any situation that might put you in a delicate position. I advise against going with your partner to any kind of reunion or get-together, which can be a risk for danger. I personally know people who left their spouse and went for a childhood sweetheart after reconnecting at a high school reunion!

Prioritize quality time with your spouse

All marriages should have two partners who feel cared for, loved, and validated. A couple should mutually depend on each other for a healthy and happy union. Those who have successful marriages do so by spending quality time with their partners without having friends, kids, or relatives involved. You should never stop dating your partner. Go out and do something special - only for the both of you - on a regular basis. It doesn't have to be a night to be remembered kind of event each time. Even spending time doing chores together in your home is one way to deeply bond. Focus on being in the moment and have fun with the person you fell head-over-heels in love with. Sometimes long-term couples get very systematic or routine about day to day tasks, and they barely talk or see one another. If you're spending a lot of time having fun with your friends instead of your partner, it can create a big space that someone else could step into. Needing too much private time puts the whole idea of being a couple in question. I can't say what is "too little" time together, but if you start to feel unconnected or unloved from your spouse, change things, and change it as quickly as possible.

Find people that will hold you accountable

If you find yourself in tempting situations as someone who struggles to be faithful, find people to hold you accountable. It's not an option but a must. These are people who encourage you to be a better person and call you out when you make a mistake. They will not tolerate your sins because they know that you're better than that. This person can be a family member, close friend, or a church group. Whoever you decide to make you accountable, make sure you always accept the responsibility for your actions and understand that they care.

Reserve time for intimacy

Both of you feel lonely and isolated. The best way to make sure you and your partner never become tempted to find intimacy in others is by making sure you are intimate with each other. Most people anticipate sex when they hear the word, intimacy, but the meaning is so much deeper. It means simply being in their presence, sharing kisses, and holding hands.

If you both are busy, don't be afraid to schedule an intimate night. It might be as simple as making out and a few hours of cuddling while watching a movie and doing little naughty things such as quickies, but it will ensure that both of you feel wanted and loved inside your marriage or relationship.

Also, take those little moments to kiss your partner good morning when they wake up and goodbye before work because it's the little things that count. These small gestures add up. Sometimes infidelity happens out of vengeful or angry feelings. Perhaps both of you feel lonely and isolated**,** and you have been going through a rough period for a long time.

It's rampant for a husband or wife to seek consolation and comfort from a friend. If that friend makes you feel appreciated, there's a chance you can be tempted. Of course, it's better if you and your partner work things out. If things are unhappy or tense for a while, face the issues. Don't run from them and work them out together. Seek counseling to help restore your relationship if you can't do it alone.

Dress up occasionally and wear something nice or sexy. Wear something you know your partner loves to see you in an intimate manner. Say, "I am so lucky I married you", "I love you" and other mushy sentiments like that. Create a candlelight dinner in your home, turn the music up high and the lights down low. This never goes out of style. Don't allow your partner to fantasize about a moonlit night on a tropical island with anyone else because they're sure you'd never be willing to do such a thing.

Learn to apologize and forgive

Holding onto grudges, resentment, and anger will tear your marriage apart even if there's no third party or affair present. When you do something wrong in your marriage, swallow your pride and ask for forgiveness. When they commit an act that hurts you, learn how to forget and forgive. Forgiving might not mean that you fully trust them again, but it's a choice you choose that says, "I'll work in making our relationship as better and sturdier than it should be." It is a way to show your husband/wife that you are committed to making your marriage work, no matter what happens. It helps to protect against infidelity because both partners now feel they can argue with each other.

Keep lines of communication open

Conversing openly with your partner is one of the best ways to avoid infidelity and reduce cheating in marriage. You should always feel comfortable and satisfied with speaking with your partner. This means sharing concerns without serious arguments and being open to difficult conversations. If you think "he/she's too old for that sort of thing" or "he/she is not the kind of person who would do such a thing", you could be mistaken. Your spouse might not intend to seek sexual satisfaction in another person's arms, but if you starve a person long enough, they'll eat anything.

Express your needs

One of the main reasons why many couples have affairs is because they feel that their emotional and physical needs are not being satisfied. Having someone outside your marriage will not fill these needs in the way you expect, so it's important to deal with the situation you're currently facing with your spouse. Tell your partner when your needs are being satisfied and give them easy action items to help you feel good.

For example, if you feel that your spouse isn't giving you enough attention, ask your spouse to reserve a date night twice a week with you. Your spouse can't fix the problem if you don't communicate, so you have to say when you are having one.

You don't have to be sexy or look young. No matter how many years you've been married, you need to watch your hygiene, comb your hair, avoid bad breath, brush your teeth, and keep yourself looking as fit and fuckable. Don't limit yourself to dressing up in fancy clothing every once in a while and then to go out for a romantic evening. Attention to such matters all the time shows your attractiveness and how alluring you can be to your partner. It helps keeps his or her eyes off someone else.

Adultery might be increasing, but that does not mean that you and your spouse will be one with it. By following these steps, you will create a marriage with a solid, robust foundation that holds up strong against infidelity. You will not need to worry because you know your both your needs are being met, and communication is effective. One of the first thing that registers in our thoughts is that it's always helpful to seek the guidance and support of a larger community and make yourself accountable to others who will hold you to a high standard of morality and marital commitment. Many churches offer support groups or adult Sunday School classes designed specifically to help couples build stronger marriages. It's a great idea to get connected with one of these classes or groups and make it a regular part of your lives.

One of the tools we've developed to help strengthen marriages is an online check-up. This assessment tool is an in-depth set of questions that will bring out the areas where you shine as a couple, as well as help you target spots that could use a little improvement – whether you're dating, engaged, newly married, or celebrating decades of life together.

Chapter 9:
Meditation for Healing

Loving-Kindness Meditation

Loving-Kindness Meditation is a practice that is meditatively used for feelings of compassion and loving-kindness to be cultivated; it is used primarily in the Theravada Buddhist tradition. Research on LKM has been inclined since the 2000s to include treatment for enhancing relationships, increase empathy and depression. It's positive effects on the research subjects have included a decrease in judgments, anxiety, fear, helplessness, emotional pain, and anger, and increases in self-efficacy, well-being, compassion, openness, and happiness.

Meditation, in general, has been proved to be effective in helping people's various illnesses, anxiety, chronic pain, and to self-regulate stress, but LKM is an open-hearted and focused approach specifically directed to feelings of compassion.

It could prove significantly beneficial in the treatment of infidelity during the last stage: Stage 3 of the Integrated Treatment Model. In research conducted by Pruitt and McCollum, the participants reported that traits of compassion and acceptance developed through the practice of loving-kindness related to "an understanding of the shared humanity of people."

Consequently, clients may be able to reconnect with their spouses in a more genuine way and empathize with their partners' struggles. Hill stated that "human forgiveness is not doing something but discovering something - that I am more like those who have hurt me than different from them."

Moreover, in the practice of Loving-Kindness Meditation, the seed of compassion implanted allows a person to be less critical of himself or herself. This is important because the practice emphasizes that before we can extend feelings of compassion and loving-kindness towards others, we shall also extend that feeling toward our selves.

According to the involved participants who were asked to practice Loving-kindness Meditation in a study examining meditation practices on intimate relationships, it was easier for them to extend acceptance or compassion to others when they first offered it to themselves. In fact, participants reported four primary meditation personalities that developed as a result of the practice; this included awareness, compassion and loving-kindness, acceptance, and disidentification from emotions and thoughts.

With the development of these personality types, the participants or volunteers found they were more willing to be present in a moment of difficult emotions. Consequently, this change in the relationship enabled them to approach external situations differently. Loving-kindness Meditation also provided participants with the understanding that people's behaviors have different reasons.

Likewise, they also reported being less responsive and more aware of their vulnerabilities from an emotional perspective. In practicing Loving-Kindness Meditation, the counselor asked each client to direct feelings of warmth and caring toward themselves intentionally so they might experience compassion for themselves. This resulted in the extension of compassion towards both of partners.

Encouraging positive feelings by practicing Loving-Kindness Meditation, in and out of session, may help reduce self-judgments and critical thoughts. When one is loving and compassionate towards the self, one can become more forgiving.

Chapter 10:
Do's and Don'ts After Discovering Infidelity

Mistakes you need to avoid at all cost

Mistake #1: Do not recklessly talk about your partner's infidelity with friends and family.

What?! Don't talk about it? You may be wondering why I offer you this kind of advice, right off the bat, because many of us are taught that talking about our problems will help us. While that may be true in most cases, I must caution you against spilling your guts about your partner's infidelity while you are still reeling in shock, anger, and pain.

Mistake #2: Do not rush to make significant, life-changing decisions right away

I realize this advice might not be ideal for all couples, depending on the level of commitment to recovery and the specifics of the situation. However, for many couples, postponing your major life-changing decisions for at least 12 months provides you with some time to gain clarity about the situation, even if you end up leaving the relationship down the road.

Mistake #3: Demanding explicit details of a sex addict

Do not demand explicit details about the betrayal. If you recently discovered your partner's sex addiction, it can be almost impossible to avoid asking for some of the dirty details because you need to know the depths of your partner's sickness and betrayal.

There's also a fine line between what you need to know and the circumstances that caused you additional pain unnecessarily. Remember, once those details are in your head, it is almost impossible to forget them. For many spouses and partners of sex addicts, this is one of the most challenging mistakes to avoid when dealing with the trauma of betrayal.

Mistake #4: Failing to set boundaries

Do not fail to set reasonable boundaries. Boundaries are rules for the relationship. Crossing the other's boundaries means you have broken the rules set in place. There are mixed opinions on the setting of limits. I know that some spouses and partners in recovery feel that boundary-setting is a disguised attempt to control the cheater.

In some cases, this is true. If you find yourself setting boundaries that require the cheater to report their every move or else they must deal with the consequences you've set, you may need to rethink your underlying reasons for setting those boundaries. Of course, you are trying to protect yourself, and that is entirely normal and understandable. But are your limits to an attempt to control the cheater by keeping constant tabs on him? Healthy boundaries are an effort to keep the lines of honest communication open between. For instance, setting a limit that requires you both to practice honesty with each other at all times is usually healthier than setting a limitation that requires the other to explain his whereabouts every time he leaves the house.

Mistake #5: Pain mining

You should not torture yourself by continuing to look for pain. The term "pain mining" does not describe the first remembrance of something unpleasant because sometimes those initial thoughts unexpectedly pop into your head without warning. Pain mining begins once you have that first painful thought or memory. After the unpleasant feeling comes to mind, you always indulge in pain mining because you are forced to drop everything else in your life to search for other things that cause additional emotional pain.

You can go from one hurtful thought to another, replaying stuff your partner told you over and over in your head. Then those memories lead you to create awful scenarios in your mind, like imagining your husband engaging in one or more of his betrayals. Once you are entirely devastated by these thoughts, you will start to look for evidence of more deceptions on their computer or written in their private journal. You end up wasting hours upon hours of your life indulging in pain mining.

Be prepared for the pain. A few points will help to turn the page.

1. **Relational Trauma**. At this point, you may feel as if the person who betrayed you has taken everything away from you. Your sense of self has probably been shattered. You could be feeling a wide variety of emotions as your heart has been broken. You might feel rage toward the person who is stealing your companion and lover away from you. You might feel deeply hurt and not be able to put words to what you are feeling.

    You might feel scared. You could be scared about the future or even feel afraid about the present. What will happen to the kids? Will I have to start dating again and go through this all over again? What if I can't trust anybody anymore? Why did this happen? Simply not knowing what to do or what will come up can be terrifying.

It is essential at this time to recognize precisely how traumatic this experience is for you. Emotionally, this is very similar to post-traumatic stress disorder (PTSD), except it could be happening right now and it also continues to happen instead of just being an experience in the past.

Psychologists and healthcare professionals suggest that getting the help you need as soon as possible is vital to prevent developing long-term post-traumatic stress disorder or so that the symptoms do not worsen. These symptoms can take hold of your life and thoroughly shake it. But with time, professional help, and taking care of yourself, complete healing and peace are possible.

2. Talk to Someone

On the path to healing, you will have to communicate with someone. At first, it may be difficult to find someone you feel you can trust who won't judge you or the situation. Those around you may be unhealthy to talk to. These are the people who leave you feeling drained and discouraged after the conversation. They will continuously tell you their opinions rather than listening and offering healthy lectures. You will know these people by how you feel during and after the conversations. They may not intentionally try to make you feel this way, but some people are not good at conversing and listening. It is a skill that needs to be developed because very few are "born with it."

The goal is to locate the persons who have uplifting words for you and who listen to what you say. These are the people who help answer your questions by giving you their ears and allowing you to follow a good train of thought, leading you to your solution. The conversations you have with these people will leave you feeling empowered and energized, and you will feel yourself letting go a little bit at a time. This will take time, but it is crucial to have someone to talk to. Do not try to go through this all by yourself.

3. **Journaling**

Journaling is a powerful tool on the path to healing. A study was conducted in which three groups of individuals were being treated for varying degrees of depression. They were each given a different kind of therapy. The three different types were talk therapy, psychotropic medication, and journaling therapy.

> The journaling group was given the task of writing for ten minutes every day. It didn't matter what they wrote; they were just told to write as if no one would ever read what they wrote. It could be thrown in the trash or burned after they had written it.
>
> After six months, the talk therapy group showed improvement, and the psychotropic medication group was right where they started six months earlier. The journaling group healed and got over their depression the fastest. The healing power that writing can unleash is unmatched in many cases.
>
> If at any point you find yourself holding back your writing and you are not allowing yourself to write what you want to, ask

yourself why. If it is because you are afraid someone will see what you have written? If that is the case, then burn or throw away your paper when you are done. Or keep it under lock and key. All that matters is that you don't hold back.

4. Enjoy nature

Using nature for healing is sometimes called green therapy, ecopsychology, or ecotherapy. This type of therapy is used for many different emotional and traumatic situations as it has been found to be very helpful for most people. Many researchers worldwide agree that having a connection to nature can better a person's emotional well-being and interpersonal relationships. The whole idea is to be removed from your office or the walls of your home you are in every day and be in the outdoors. This is done to develop an emotional bond with yourself and nature.

Psychologists say that when a person finds this connection with nature, they experience feelings of stability, harmony, timelessness, and balance. Many sudden feel a sense of something bigger outside of themselves when they find this connection. It requires them to recognize a higher power, which is necessary for the healing process.

Nature is the strand that binds everyone together. We all live on this good Earth. Often, we forget about life and the natural beauty that abounds. A stroll in the park or a drive in the country can be very healing. The grandeur of the earth can help us put our lives in perspective. Our lives can seem quite small when taking in the vast beauty that is nature. The sting of our pain can be swallowed up when we allow ourselves to enjoy something as broad as nature.

I remember talking to a wilderness survival expert once who said, "In a wilderness survival situation, you find out that no matter who you are or how much money you make, nature does things her own way; she doesn't respect anyone." It is true how insignificant we are.

Nature allows us to see that the world goes on. Usually, after a betrayal or traumatic event, we would like the world to stop so we can take a time out. Unfortunately, it doesn't stop, but WE tend to stay. It is a lot like standing in a river and the water (or the world) keeps moving around us. Mostly, if we are not moving forward, then everything else is moving around us. There are many lessons and things we can learn from nature. I'll leave those for you to discover on your journey.

5. Find Something to Laugh at

Laughter is the best medicine. Scientifically it has been shown to reduce anxiety and stress. It is incredibly beneficial in helping cancer patients cope with the constant pain of some treatments. The bottom line is that it has many applications in the medical field, and grief is a type of pain. Our job is to make that pain go away in a real and meaningful way.

Chapter 11:
The Trust Rebuilding Process of Healing from Infidelity

Trust is perhaps the most important element in a successful, happy, and long-lasting relationship. Being able to trust our partners gives us an inherent sense of safety and makes us comfortable being open and honest when revealing our true selves.

Trust can be broken by a number of things, such as infidelity, broken promises, or untruths. But if these things happen in your relationship, does it necessarily mean it's the end?

If you and your partner are truly committed to rebuilding your broken relationship, it can be done. Acknowledge that if trust has been lost, the journey back can be a long one – but it is possible. It requires both parties to commit to reconnecting with each other and picking up the pieces of their relationship.

Fully understand the situation

If you are the one who was betrayed, to re-establish trust in your partner, it is important that you first understand the exact situation that led to the trust being broken. What happened, when and where? What were the circumstances? Why do you think this happened? The aim here is not to make judgements, simply to view the situation from an objective, fact-based point of view.

If you are the partner who did the betraying, your duty here is to be as open and honest as possible, providing your partner with answers to all their questions.

Letting go of your anger

While this can certainly be easier said than done, it is important to take note of the effect anger can have on both your mental and physical well-being. Prolonged anger can lead to increased anxiety, high blood pressure, and frequent headaches, as well as poor sleep, diminished appetite, and mental stress.

To let go of the anger you are holding inside, you must first become fully aware of it. What emotions might you have bottled up or refused to confront? What was the exact effect of your partner's betrayal? Did it trigger feelings of abandonment or lack of self-worth? Did you feel as though you were made a fool of? Becoming fully aware of these feelings is an important step in releasing them. Now communicate these feelings to your partner in a calm and rational manner.

This is a chance that the partner who did the betraying will share their feelings. Likely, their poor behavior was triggered by negative emotions or beliefs, and they may be carrying around a similar amount of anger. It is just as crucial for the offender to identify their emotions to release them and prevent any further breaches of trust.

Make your partner aware of your commitment

When trust is broken, it can lead both the betrayer and the betrayed to question their partner's commitment to rebuilding the relationship. If you have been betrayed, you may question whether your partner was committed to you in the first place; and if you were the offending party, you might consider whether your actions were too grievous for your partner to come back from.

But if there is to be a true rebuilding of trust, it is crucial that both parties reaffirm their commitment. This is a chance for the betrayer to convey their regret or remorse, along with any other feelings they may be experiencing, such as frustration. And it is an opportunity for the betrayed to be open about their hurt. As you share your feelings, try to do so from a place of empathy. Consider how your partner is feeling in this moment and do your best to support them.

From here, both parties must articulate what they need from the relationship to move forward. Do this in a calm and respectful manner, using non-blaming language such as, "I need to feel loved" rather than "You made me feel unloved." Once you reach this step, the time for blaming is behind you, and it's important your statements reflect that.

Decide to forgive – or allow yourself to be forgiven

Remember that a big part of forgiveness is actively deciding to do so, choosing to no longer wish ill-luck upon the partner who has betrayed you. Conversely, if you are the one who has committed the offense, you may find it a challenge to allow yourself to be forgiven; in other words, you may find it difficult to forgive yourself for your actions. Because, while forgiving others can be a challenge, forgiving ourselves, particularly when we have committed an offense that has hurt our partner or put our relationship in jeopardy, can be much more difficult. Thanks to our inner critic – that negative voice we all have inside our heads, criticizing us and pointing out our failures– we have the tendency to replay negative events over and over. This causes us to dwell on our mistakes and punish ourselves far more harshly than we likely would if another person had behaved in the same manner.

Forgiving ourselves requires many of the same skills as forgiving others, specifically, compassion, kindness and understanding, but it can be much more difficult to give these things to ourselves than offer them to others. But if you and your partner are to rebuild trust and move on, forgiving yourself is crucial.

This is for a number of reasons, including the need for release. When we are able to forgive ourselves, we release the physical tension we have been carrying inside our bodies, a tension that, just like prolonged anger, can cause stress that leads to many physical and mental ailments.

Forgiving ourselves also increases our capacity to forgive others. We are unable to give away that which we don't have. If we are unable to forgive ourselves for our mistakes, it becomes much harder to forgive others. Think of the long-lasting effect this can have on your relationship. How can you move forward if you are in a place where you would be unable to forgive your partner for any mistakes?

Forgiveness allows us to grow. When we forgive ourselves and learn to move past our mistakes, we can reframe the past and learn from it instead of punishing ourselves repeatedly. Our mistakes then become a source of growth that strengthens the relationship rather than destroy it.

Acknowledge and accept your emotions. The first step in moving past our mistakes is acknowledging our emotions. Take time to recognize exactly what it is you are feeling. Let your emotions rise to the surface, however painful they are, and give them a name. Are you disappointed in yourself? Angry? Frustrated? By acknowledging exactly what it is we are feeling, we have a firm starting point to forgive ourselves and repair our relationship with both our partners and ourselves.

Acknowledge the lesson at hand. Any failures in life can be viewed as opportunities to learn. So too can situations in which you feel the need for self-forgiveness. You have acknowledged the facts of your mistake and discussed it openly with your partner. This may have been difficult, but it was likely also quite therapeutic. Now consider what you can take away from the situation? Perhaps it led you to recognize your need for more freedom within the relationship or a deep-seated fear of being abandoned. How will understanding these things help you move forward in your relationship and develop as a person?

Connect with your inner critic. That voice inside our heads is constantly criticizing us and making us question our abilities. Not only can this inner critic cause us to constantly doubt ourselves, but it is also the voice inside that tells us we do not deserve to be forgiven. All too often, we attempt to silence our inner critic by attempting to ignore it, believing this is the only way to move past its destructive words. But connecting and conversing with this negative voice can actually be far more helpful.

Begin to become aware of the thoughts that arise as your inner critic begins to speak. Can you identify the ways in which you are self-sabotaging your happiness and chance for forgiveness? For each comment your inner critic makes, do your best to analyze it in an objective way. How true is this observation? For example, if your inner voice tells you, "You've ruined your marriage, and you'll never find happiness again," is this necessarily true? It may feel like it at times, but if you examine the situation from a more objective, level-headed viewpoint, you will see that it is, in fact, a lie. You and your partner are working to repair your broken relationship, and when you do so, it will lead you to happiness again.

For each self-destructive thought, try and replace it with a more compassionate and constructive response. For the above example, you may replace the above statement with, "We are rebuilding our marriage and finding happiness along the way."

Give yourself time. It may be that you are simply not ready to process the necessary emotions right now. Perhaps the negative emotions your mistake has aroused are threatening to overwhelm you, and you don't feel you have the strength to work through your pain. If you see yourself positioned like this, first of all, take a moment to accept that this is all right. Don't use the situation as yet another excuse to punish or convince yourself the relationship is over. Acknowledge that you made a mistake and will work through it in the near future when you are in a better frame of mind. Then, to stop yourself from dwelling on the negativity and from roiling away inside you, imagine removing the negative emotions from your body and locking them in a box. Now picture yourself putting the box away somewhere safe. Give yourself permission to leave the box and the feelings within it to one side for now, with the knowledge that you will return to it when you feel you are ready.

Avoid dwelling on the past. As we now know, a big part of forgiveness is consciously choosing to do so. When forgiving others, we choose to no longer wish them ill will and make the shift to a place of compassion and kindness. Similarly, when we forgive ourselves, we need to make a conscious decision to no longer beat ourselves up over our offense. If you continue to dwell on your mistakes, it can have a negative effect on your relationship.

But not dwelling on the past is certainly easier said than done. As humans, we have a tendency to focus on our errors and torture ourselves by replaying our mistakes over and over in our heads. This is especially true if our mistakes have put our marriages or relationships in jeopardy or caused great harm to the one we love.

To stop yourself from constantly replaying the mistakes in your head, it is first important to recognize you are doing it. Often these thoughts and negative experiences churn through our minds, so automatically, we are not aware of them - just of the negative feelings they evoke. When you catch yourself thinking of the past, stop and take note of it. Acknowledge exactly what thoughts are in your head and how they are making you feel. Now, instead of allowing yourself to continue to dwell on the experience, replace it with positive action.

Chapter 12: Healing from Infidelity in LGBTQ Couples

For LGBTQ couples who want to heal their relationships after an affair, there is good reason to be hopeful. Although the results of studies vary, most research reveals that two-thirds of heterosexual couples will remain together after an affair. While the research on this topic among gay couples is limited, most indicate that LGBT couples are even more likely to recover from affairs. Of course, some of these couples may stay together in misery, while others will truly improve their relationships.

How can you and your partner grow as a couple after an affair?

It takes time

After a period of time, the partner who had an affair will want the conversation to end. They'll get tired of hearing how they hurt their partner. They'll get impatient with the process and want to move on. They may feel like they are being punished. However, if they want to repair the relationship, they will need to tolerate the slow process of healing. They will need to practice the art of patience and understanding.

The partner who feels betrayed needs to practice expressing and naming their feelings again and again. Their job is to identify their range of feelings and then communicate them clearly and respectfully. Attacking their partner and seeking revenge won't move the process forward.

They need to become fully aware of their feelings and ask and expect that their feelings will be heard and respected.

Here is the bottom line: we all want to be heard. It may be the most important experience we are seeking in a relationship. So relationship recovery is a listening process.

It's uncomfortable

None of this is easy territory. It is best done with what therapists call a strong container. This could be a couples counseling office, or it could be on your living room couch with the phone turned off, plenty of eye contact, and a shared commitment to key rules of communication.

Perhaps the single most important communication rule is to speak from the "I" position. Rather than complaining, focus on how you feel when your partner do cheats. This approach avoids escalating the argument because how can someone debate what you feel. You are the only expert on your feelings. Sharing feelings in this manner leads to empathy, and that leads to healing.

Don't waste a good crisis

Often, the crisis of an affair becomes an opportunity to look at and improve some of the ongoing issues within the relationship. It's commonly the wake-up call that gets both partners motivated to do the scary work of speaking truthfully.

Affairs, untreated addictions and poor self-care habits are all methods of attempted escape. They help us avoid the worthwhile and challenging work of looking at what is really true about ourselves, our childhood experiences, and our relationships. They represent "acting out" of feelings rather than directly facing them with mindfulness and compassionate courage.

When we escape our partners and ourselves with any hurtful behaviors, we can expect to injure people we love. Exploring our underlying, more vulnerable feelings is the essential recipe for healing our relationships with others, as well as our relationship with ourselves.

Focuses on the healing process

I have walked the dark and dangerous paths. I closed myself off and didn't trust anyone for years. These are my regrets. I don't regret the lying, the cheating, and the pain because I learned from these things, and I grew stronger. I regret that I let myself down by closing myself off. I lost years. And for what? For whom? Honestly, I am more than a little angry at having allowed someone to turn my life upside down like that. It wasn't so much cheating as the time that followed the cheating. Looking back, I cannot believe that I let myself down like that. I don't like the person I was. That is on me; that is my fault. I started my healing process years too late. The years I spent reliving it all was so stupid of me. But having finally opened my eyes, I am trying to see the silver lining. I have accepted my mistakes, and have healed myself, and now I show you the way.

You must learn to accept yourself unconditionally. Unconditional self-acceptance is a belief - a belief in one's self. Each belief includes what we think of ourselves, how we evaluate ourselves, and so forth. They are effective and connotative components. So, unconditional acceptance of the self means we believes that we must accept ourselves, regardless of how we think, feel, or behave in any current, past or future context. This is the acceptance of self without conditionality, without imposed or self-imposed conditions, standards or imperatives that we mistakenly think we must accomplish before we can find love and appreciation.

The main goal

Unconditional self-acceptance as a concept sounds simple, but in practice, achieving this goal is a time-consuming and difficult process. Why? Because all of us, from an early age, have been taught, both within the family and in social settings, that we "must" think, feel, and behave in a certain way, in certain situations (usually the way our parents taught us); and if we don't behave in that manner, then we are bad people.

That's not a way of thinking healthily. Since every child is eager for love, attention and acceptance, each of us has learned and adopted certain standards and norms of behavior that we adhere to as an adult. Those standards are of social origin and common to all of us who live in the same society and the same culture. Yet we are all different.

Values, ideals, and desirable life goals are forged in different families and vary accordingly. For example, in some families, the importance of schooling is emphasized, while in others it is about acquiring wealth. It may include the importance of community, family life, and religion when we are grown and our personalities are formed. We are able to (and regularly do) set different standards, life goals, and norms of behavior. When we adhere to these adopted or self-constructed standards, we find that everything is fine, and we have no reason to reject and disrespect ourselves as persons. But when we break these standards, many of us will reject ourselves. This attitude toward one's self necessarily brings suffering, depression, fear, guilt and shame.

Remember this

An opposite extreme would be an uncritical attitude towards one's self and others. By accepting a complete lack of any norms of behavior, recklessness towards others, selfishness, an absence of any respect for others, the absence of feelings of guilt, and even brutality, we become psychopaths. The people prone to accepting rejection and self-defeat are the people we call neurotic. These individuals are harmful to themselves, while psychopaths are harmful and dangerous to others and to society as a whole.

Since we know this to be true, we must seek normalcy, a middle ground, in order to achieve what we call mental health. We must learn how to accept ourselves unconditionally, even when we misbehave.

Just accept the facts

It should be easy for us to love, appreciate, and accept ourselves, to be proud of ourselves and happy when we behave according to the standards we have set for ourselves—standards we regard as just and socially acceptable. But what happens when we fail to meet those standards, in whole or in part? What if we fail to achieve our goals, hurt someone, make mistakes, act selfishly, leave a loved one, feel depressed, desperate, angry, scared, or ashamed? How then do we unconditionally accept ourselves in such situations? How can we love, value and respect ourselves as persons?

What forms the core of unconditional self-acceptance is exactly that! We accept ourselves in all situations, no matter what happens, or how we feel, think and behave. Does this imply an uncritical attitude towards one's behavior and actions? Not at all!!! It is desirable and useful to be critical of our actions, thoughts, and feelings but not of ourselves as whole persons.

You can learn this

People can learn to accept themselves unconditionally by first learning to distinguish between what they think, feel, and do as individuals. One must first ask if there are good and bad people? The answer is clear; they do not exist because if they exist, it will mean that good people have always acted well, correctly, and infallibly in every situation in the past and will always do so in the future. Bad people will always do the opposite. This is, of course, a ridiculous concept. If I did something wrong, does it necessarily follow that I am a bad person overall; only my behavior was bad? Conversely, if I do some action that qualify as good, that does not mean that I am an entirely good person. What happens when I make a mistake? Does my car having bad tires necessarily mean that my entire car is bad and ready for the junkyard? So, to think that you are bad because occasionally you make mistakes does not qualify you as a bad person. Such a conclusion is illogical and a mistake of overgeneralization. Think about it, are you judging other people based on one or more behaviors. If you do this, your appraisals are very imprecise.

Be critical and objective

So, be critical of your behavior, your actions, your misguided patterns of thinking and feeling, but don't think you are a bad person for it. All of us are imperfect and sinful beings, committing sins, but not sinners by definition. Sinners are those who perceive their actions as bad, but they continue to behave that way because they receive some benefit from such behavior.

Therefore, you can be strict with regard to your actions, and you can feel regret and remorse, but not guilt and self-hatred when you do something wrong. Regret and remorse will motivate you to change your behavior and strive to correct it in the future. But guilt and self-hatred will destroy you. So, scold yourself if you act badly sometimes. But limit it to that.

Problems arise when the conditions people set for themselves are not met. If, as a result, we make the wrong conclusions, and we are not worthy to accept ourselves and to love and be loved, then we cannot be happy in our lives. This attitude can be expressed in the sentence, "If I have failed to accomplish this and that, if I have made mistakes in the past, if I am not loved to the extent that I want to be loved, then I cannot love myself, I am bad, unworthy or even worthless." It is this attitude that leads to suffering, failure, and unhappy existence.

Don't be like this...

I've said that this way of thinking is irrational, harmful, and dangerous to ourselves and our self-confidence. As long as we hold such irrational beliefs, we will never love and appreciate ourselves, and those who cannot love and appreciate themselves cannot love and appreciate others. By adhering to such beliefs, we are condemned to lifelong discontent, suffering, and unhappiness. If you are prone to such attitudes, I ask you where is the benefit? What have you achieved? Can you become a better person by hating and belittling yourself? Certainly not! It only creates additional suffering and pain. Life provides enough suffering and pain. Creating our own is not necessary at all.

And finally, be critical of your behavior, your thoughts, and your feelings, but be flexible and take the position of unconditionally accepting yourself. Do your best to change everything you find objectionable in yourself, but never condemn yourself. Learn to forgive yourself so that you can forgive others because we are all sinners; humans are imperfect beings. Tell yourself, "If I were wrong, I would try to fix it, and I will do my best not to repeat the mistake. Being wrong does not mean you are a sinner or a bad person. Your personality and your identity are much broader than your actions, which you may certainly change. Be consistent in this new way of treating yourself. If you find yourself in a disparaging and self-defeating moment, pause and ask yourself if it benefits you. Is it logical? By consistently opposing irrational ideas about yourself, you will gradually learn to be more flexible, successful, and self-sufficient. You will learn to respect and love yourself and will transfer that confidence to other people.

I wanted you to know that you can learn to love again. That is not a problem, and it will happen over time, but you must unconditionally accept yourself. You must realize that you are perfect just the way you are, and please don't overthink everything. Don't repeat my mistakes. Just relax and realize that life is to be lived. It's all worth it in the end. Trust me!

Cheating is not the end of a relationship

Some people think that cheating is the end of a marriage. It is simply not true. Although healing from infidelity is tough work, most relationships not only survive, but they actually grow and get stronger from an unfortunate experience.

I am not saying that cheating is good for marriages. Infidelity is very destructive because the bond of trust has been shattered. However, it is possible to get relationships back on track and rediscover trust, caring, love, friendship, desire and pleasure.

Infidelity can be found in any misdeed. When two persons are married, they must care for and nourish each other's feelings. They must behave in a manner that makes the relationship feel safe and progressive.

Consequently, if one partner feels threatened or betrayed, the other partner must do some thorough soul searching and change to house those feelings. In summary, infidelity is in the eye of the beholder. Change and ensure you make the marriage work.

Chapter 13:
Tips for Re-building Trust with your Partner

Infidelity involves the direct breaking of trust. The immoral act that you cannot share with a spouse because you know it would hurt him/her is breakage.

For a couple to heal a relationship after infidelity, they have to learn to tell the truth (more so for the cheater) actively. If there is something one person wants to know, the other should be willing to open up. The offender should always volunteer valuable information as soon as possible. The betrayed spouse is already angry because of the infidelity, but he/she will be angrier if the partner keeps secrets. Even a little thing that looks suspicious might bring about emotions and denial.

Unfortunately, the offender might mess up during the healing process in numerous ways even though he/she is willing to work on the relationship. Some of the pitfalls can involve:

Passive truth-telling. Passive truth-telling will force the betrayed partner to handle all the hard and investigative work. If the betrayed partner feels suspicious that the spouse has done something wrong, he/she must ask. The offender might answer the question but fail to offer other valuable information. However, the betrayed partner might have some of the missing information and will tell when he/she is fed half-truths. A cheater will sometimes try to convince him/herself that he/she is no longer cheating because he/she is not lying or covering up as much as before. Failing to disclose all useful information is another form of lying is a shame.

Partial disclosure. The majority of cheater will tell only a part of the truth or tell outright lies to the betrayed partner. Typically, this partial disclosure will lead to the couple revealing to each other some information today, another tomorrow, the following day, etc. Over time, it becomes very painful for the betrayed partner, besides rereading havoc in the process of rebuilding trust.

The child's role. In this case, the offender plays the child, whereby he/she tells the betrayed partner, "There is something I need to tell you" then waits for the other person to ask, "What is it?" or "Is that all?" or "Are you sure that is all?" Instead of restoring the relationship, such an inquisition turn honesty into an investigation.

Minimizing. Sometimes, a cheater is rigorously honest, but at the same time, he/she is trying to de-escalate or dismiss or minimize the reactions of their betrayed partners. They even do this out of love and pure feeling because they do not want to see their partner suffer. However, the feeling is part of the healing process for a betrayed spouse, so trying to protect him/her is pointless. The cheater initiated the pain in the first place, so he/she should allow it to take place.

Getting defensive or attacking. The majority of betrayed mates get angry when they hear the truth about the spouse's actions. As such, the cheater takes the defensive side, and when faced with danger, he/she attacks. A form of attack could be blaming the spouse having brought on the affair. Although the cheater might be justified to feel defensive, this reaction is counteractive to a relationship-building process. When and if a cheater says something like, 'Yes, but..." in response, the purpose of the conversation changes.

<u>Expecting instant forgiveness</u>. Some cheaters will be rigorously honest with the expectation that opening up will earn them instance forgiveness. In most cases, that does not work. The betrayed person has to feel the whole process of betrayal and healing before he/she can forgive fully.

The first and most important step in rebuilding trust is to be entirely honest and live in a glasshouse, where the betrayed partner can see everything happening. The partner who cheated should ensure that he/she can account for every move he/she makes in a day and tell the partner all the details. If a cheater becomes fully open without complaining or being defensive, the betrayed partner will come around gradually.

Rigorous honesty is not easy, and most people caught cheating do not like it. It can be emotionally painful for the two partners. However, they will have to bear with it because it is a large part of healing and forgiveness. The good news is that gradually, the cheated-on partner will develop confidence in the person who hurt him/her and believe that he/she is living an honest life once again.

Stages of Grief:

Denial

Once the affair is discovered, there is an initial period of denial and maybe shock. This may include believing only what you want to hear or making excuses for the betrayer. The denial may extend beyond a tolerable time, which is a perfectly normal reaction. In cases where denial extends many years, the betrayed person most likely reached acceptance and inwardly experienced all stages of grief silently but chose to live with the lies.

Anger

When the full impact of cheating and adultery hits home, pure rage sets in. Anger can be directed to the betrayer or displaced incorrectly to others, including children, work colleagues, or even God. This stage is a difficult one to pass through, and violence often becomes evident in what was a non-violent relationship.

Bargaining

Bargaining is the beginning of the decision-making process, where both or one of the parties looks at offering negotiations. These bargains or negotiations can be made with each other, with the self or with a higher being. It may include statements like "if she takes me back, I will never do that again" or "if you tell me where you are going, I might be able to trust you again."

Depression

With the reality of the affair comes the knowledge of problems within the relationship that either can or cannot be worked out. Either way, one grieves for the relationship that once was, which was less complicated and affair free. Depression has been described as a heavy cloud over your head that makes it difficult to function, enjoy life, and even get up in the morning. Depression should be carefully monitored and addressed by professionals if needed.

Acceptance

The final stage is that of acceptance. True acceptance comes when functioning has returned and acknowledgment of the incident in its entirety exists. Many people reach acceptance by forgiving all parties, including themselves. Forgiveness is like freeing oneself from all the negative feelings associated with infidelity and being able to move forward either within the relationship or external to it. Forgiving is a difficult challenge for some, and acceptance is not dependent on the ability to forgive.

Bonus Test:
The Perfect Test to Find Out if Your Partner Is Cheating on You

---

Do you think your wife is betraying you? Does your boyfriend have a lover? Find out with this test. Answer all the following questions and discover the risk of betrayal in your love relationship:

1. Has your partner recently spent more time looking after his or her physical appearance?

    Yes (1 point)

    No (0 points)

    I do not pay any attention (0 points)

2. Has your partner been more tolerant of you lately?

    Yes (0.5 points)

    No (0 points)

3. Does your partner lock some of his/her drawers?

    Yes (2 points)

    No (0 points)

4. When the phone rings, does your partner leave the room to answer it?

    Yes (1 point)

No (0 points)

5. Does your partner tell you lies?

>Yes (2 points)

>No (0 points)

>Yes, so they will not be scolded (1 point)

6. How does your partner react to your proposals?

>He or she often accepts or agrees (0 points)

>He or she often uses fatigue as a reason to refuse (1 point)

>He or she accepts but, a few times, without enthusiasm (0.5 points)

7. Your husband or wife went out, and if you asked where he or she went, he or she is vague about it.

>It never happens (0 points)

>Occasionally, but you do not investigate (0.5 points)

>Lately, it happens more frequently (1 point)

8. Have you noticed that your boyfriend or girlfriend has changed the password of his or her computer or email, or a new email account has been created in the last few months?

>No, it did not happen (0 points)

>I do not think so; maybe it was done for greater security (0 points)

Yes, it happened (1 point)

9. Has your partner recently changed his/her habits and schedules?

Yes (0.5 point)

No (0 point)

10. Does your husband or wife have mood swings, often changing from joy to sadness and vice versa?

No, it does not happen (0 points)

It has always been like this (0 points)

Lately, he has mood swings (0.5 points)

11. Does your partner have a little desire to be with you?

He or she always has the same desire, more or less (0 points)

Lately, he or she has less desire (1 point)

If we can, we prefer to do things separately, each with spaces (0.5 points)

12. If you wear a new dress, does your partner notice it?

Yes (0 point)

No (0.5 point)

13. Has your partner known and met new people?

Yes (0.5 point)

No (0 point)

14. Does your husband or wife emphasize—with jokes and gestures—your routine?

>Yes (1 point)

>No (0 points)

15. Does your partner tend to prefer group outings and feel bored when you are alone together?

>Yes (1 point)

>No (0 points)

16. Has your partner recently enrolled in a class without asking to involve you, too?

>Yes (1 point)

>No (0 points)

17. Has your husband or wife started going to the gym?

>Yes (0.5 point)

>No (0 point)

18. Is your partner often on the phone, and he or she receives SMS messages at different times?

>Yes (2 points) No (0 points)

Count the points for the answers you gave to find out if your partner is loyal to you.

From 0-9 points — you are mutually faithful and satisfied with your relationship. If it were a fairy tale, the phrase could be used, and they lived happily ever after. Until you know how to draw stimuli from your relationship, you will be happy in love. But remember that eternal love lasts for 18 months, according to statistics! It is up to you to keep the relationship alive by listening to each other and taking space and time for you, maybe doing a nice vacation from time to time.

From 10-18 points — if you do not repair your damages, routine increases the risk of infidelity. It is okay to be sure of yourself and of your relationship, but you risk taking your love for granted, and that is the first step in falling into routine and monotony, which encourage people to look for certain emotions elsewhere. Curiosity and passion must never be lacking, and the world is full of beautiful women or interesting men. Be careful.

Conclusion

Not every affair marks the end of a relationship. However, every case of infidelity will redefine a relationship. There will be anger and hurt, and both spouses will feel lost and lonely for a while. If you feel that your relationship is worth continuing and fighting for, there will be plenty of room for rediscovering and growth with the right guidance and steps.

The heartache will not always feel stronger than you can handle. Some days you will feel sad, while others you will be as strong as ever. This alteration of moods is fine because you are grieving for what you had, what you thought you were working for, and what you are losing. You are in doubt of who you thought you were. You are not sure about your spouse anymore. Everything is there, but you are wondering if it is the same. Sometimes, it is not better or worse. It is just different.

Good people make bad decisions, and anyone can be a victim of bad choices. It is hard to explain why we end up hurting the people we love the most. Sometimes, we become the people we never imagined we could be. The good thing about mistakes is that they instill in our cores new truths and wisdom that we would not necessarily know otherwise. An affair or case of infidelity is a tough time for any relationship, but it does not have to be its definition.

Rather than gathering the broken pieces and going over and over them keeping the wounds fresh, we can use what we have to make a better life for ourselves and our spouses. Knowledge is power, and it can be used to make the relationship stronger, wiser, more knowledgeable, honest, and full of sustainable love.

You hold the keys to your life. You are the one behind the wheel—nothing and no one that can change that. Everything is up to you. Never give up on yourself, certainly not because of someone else's actions. Yes, I know how much you are suffering, and I know how much you want a second chance. Always remember that every ending is a new beginning. It doesn't matter how painful the ending is. You will overcome this and become a better and stronger person. You will be better for yourself, and when you become better for yourself, you will be better for everyone else.

NOTES

www.ingramcontent.com/pod-product-compliance
Lightning Source LLC
Chambersburg PA
CBHW070501120526
44590CB00013B/712